D0457095

Start
Where You Are

OTHER BOOKS BY CHARLES R. SWINDOLL

BOOKS

Active Spirituality
The Bride
Come Before Winter
Compassion: Showing We Care in a
    Careless World
David: A Man of Passion and Destiny
Dear Graduate
Dropping Your Guard
Encourage Me
Esther: A Woman of Strength and Dignity
The Finishing Touch
Flying Closer to the Flame
For Those Who Hurt
God's Provision in Time of Need
The Grace Awakening
Growing Deep in the Christian Life
Growing Strong in the Seasons of Life
Growing Wise in Family Life
Hand Me Another Brick
Home: Where Life Makes Up Its Mind
Hope Again
Improving Your Serve
Intimacy with the Almighty
Joseph: A Man of Integrity and Forgiveness
Killing Giants, Pulling Thorns

Laugh Again
Leadership: Influence That Inspires
Living Above the Level of Mediocrity
Living Beyond the Daily Grind,
    Books I and II
The Living Insights Study Bible,
    General Editor
Living on the Ragged Edge
Make Up Your Mind
Man to Man
Moses: A Man of Selfless Dedication
Paw Paw Chuck's Big Ideas in the Bible
The Quest for Character
Recovery: When Healing Takes Time
Sanctity of Life
Simple Faith
Starting Over
Strengthening Your Grip
Stress Fractures
Strike the Original Match
The Strong Family
Suddenly One Morning
Three Steps Forward, Two Steps Back
Victory: A Winning Game Plan for Life
You and Your Child

MINIBOOKS

Abraham: A Model of Pioneer Faith
David: A Model of Pioneer Courage
Esther: A Model of Pioneer Independence

Moses: A Model of Pioneer Vision
Nehemiah: A Model of Pioneer
    Determination

BOOKLETS

Anger
Attitudes
Commitment
Dealing with Defiance
Demonism
Destiny
Divorce
Eternal Security
Forgiving and Forgetting
Fun Is Contagious!
God's Will
Hope
Impossibilities
Integrity
Leisure
The Lonely Whine of the Top Dog

Make Your Dream Come True
Making the Weak Family Strong
Moral Purity
Our Mediator
Praise . . . In Spite of Panic
Portrait of a Faithful Father
The Power of a Promise
Prayer
Reflections from the Heart: A Prayer Journal
Seeking the Shepherd's Heart
Sensuality
Stress
This is No Time for Wimps
Tongues
When Your Comfort Zone Gets the Squeeze
Woman

Start
Where You Are

Catch a Fresh Vision for Your Life

CHARLES R. SWINDOLL

WORD PUBLISHING

NASHVILLE

A Thomas Nelson Company

START WHERE YOU ARE:
CATCH A FRESH VISION FOR YOUR LIFE

Copyright © 1999 by Charles R. Swindoll, Inc.

All rights reserved.
No portion of this book may be reproduced, stored in a retrieval
system, or transmitted in any form or by any means—electronic,
mechanical, photocopy, recording, or any other—except for
brief quotations in printed reviews, without the prior
permission of the publisher.

Unless otherwise indicated, Scripture quotations used in this book
are from the New American Standard Bible NASB © 1960, 1962,
1963, 1968, 1971, 1972, 1973, 1975, 1977 by the Lockman
Foundation. Used by permission.
The King James Version of the Bible (KJV).
The Living Bible (TLB), copyright 1971
by Tyndale House Publishers, Wheaton, Ill.
Used by permission.
The Holy Bible, New International Version (NIV).
Copyright © 1973, 1978, 1984 International Bible Society.
Used by permission of Zondervan Bible Publishers.
J.B. Phillips: The New Testament in Modern English, Revised
Edition (PHILLIPS). Copyright © J. B. Phillips 1958, 1960, 1972.
Used by permission of Macmillan Publishing Co., Inc.

Library of Congress Cataloging-in-Publication Data

Swindoll, Charles R.
Start where you are : catch a fresh vision for your life /
Charles R. Swindoll
p.   cm.

ISBN 0-8499-1603-8

1. Christian life—Evangelical Free Church of America authors.
I. Title

BV4501.2.S8955   1999   99-11647
248.4' 8995—dc21   CIP

Printed in the United States of America
9 0 1 2 3 4 5 6 7 RRD 9 8 7 6 5 4 3 2 1

CONTENTS

Part Three: Keep Your Balance
Remembering Compassion in a Careless World

Part Four: Achieve Your Goals
A Game Plan for Personal Victory

Part One
Start Where You Are:

Agreeing That Healing Takes Time

*T*o start fresh, to start over, to start *anything*, you have to know where you are. To get somewhere else, it's necessary to know where you're standing right now.

That's true in a department store or in a big church, on a freeway or on a college campus . . . or in *life*, for that matter. Seldom does anybody "just happen" to end up on a right road. The process of redirecting our lives is often painful, slow, and even confusing.

Occasionally, it seems unbearable.

Consider Jonah, one of the most prejudiced, bigoted, openly rebellious, and spiritually insensitive prophets in Scripture. Other prophets ran to the Lord; he ran *from* Him. Others declared the promises of God with fervor and zeal. Not Jonah. He was about as motivated as a six-hundred-pound grizzly in mid-January.

Somewhere down the line, the prophet got his inner directions cross-wired. He wound up, of all places, in a ship on the Mediterranean Sea bound for a place named Tarshish. That was due west. God had told him *Nineveh*. That was due east. (That's like flying from Los Angeles to Berlin by way of Honolulu.) But Jonah never got to Tarshish, as you may remember. Through a traumatic chain of events, Jonah began to get his head together in the digestive tract of a gigantic fish.

What a place to start! Sloshing around in the seaweed and juices of the monster's stomach, fishing for a match to find his way out, Jonah took a long, honest look at his short, dishonest life. He yelled for mercy. He recited psalms. He promised the Lord that he would keep his vow and get back on target. Only one creature on earth felt sicker than Jonah—the fish, in whose belly Jonah bellowed. Up came the prophet, who hit the road running—*toward Nineveh.*

THE BLESSING OF NEW

One of the most encouraging things about new years, new weeks, new days, and new opportunities is the word *new.* Friend Webster reveals its meaning: "refreshed, different from one of the same that has existed previously; unfamiliar."

Best of all, it's a place to start again.

To catch a fresh vision.

To change directions.

To begin a new phase of your life's journey.

But that requires knowing where you are. It requires taking time to honestly admit your present condition. It means facing the music, standing alone inside the fish and coming to terms with whatever needs attention, nosing around in the seaweed for a match. Before you find your way out, you must determine where you are. Only once that is accomplished are you ready to start (or restart) your journey.

Consider what the prophet Joel writes to all the Jonahs (or Joans) who may have picked up this book. God is speaking: "I will make up to you for the years that the swarming locust has eaten, the creeping locust, the stripping locust, and the gnawing locust" (Joel 2:25).

If God can take a disobedient prophet, turn him around, and set him on fire spiritually, He can do the same with you. He is a Specialist at making something useful and beautiful out of something broken and confused.

Where are you, friend? *Start there.* Openly and freely declare your need to the One who cares deeply. Don't hide a thing. Show God all of those locust bites. He's ready to heal every one . . . if you're ready to run toward that Nineveh called *tomorrow.*[1]

Where are you, friend? Start there.

Chapter 1

ADMITTING NEED

> A prayer to be said
> When the world has gotten you
> down,
> And you feel rotten,
> And you're too doggone tired to
> pray,
> And you're in a big hurry,
> And besides, you're mad at
> everybody...
> *HELP!*

There it was ... one of those posters. Some are funny. Some are clever. A few thought-provoking. This one? Convicting. God really wanted me to get the message.

He nudged me when I first read it in an administrator's office at a conference center in northern California. He slapped me hard when I ran into it again in a shop at Newport Beach. While moving faster than a speeding bullet through a publishing firm in Portland, I came face to face with it again, silent as light but twice as bright ... smashing me down and pinning me to the mat for the full count. It was almost as if I could hear His celestial voice saying, "My son, slow down. Cool it. Admit your needs."

Start Where You Are   1

Such good counsel. Ah, but so tough to carry out!

Which begs a question. If asking for help is so smart—especially when we're about to launch into a new leg of our life's journey—why don't we?

The reason is as sad as it is foolish. It comes down to plain, unvarnished pride, a stubborn unwillingness to admit our need. It's been bred into us by that insistent inner voice which urges us on: *Prove it to 'em! You can do it . . . and you don't need anybody's help.*

The result? Impatience. Irritation. Anger. Longer hours. Less and less laughter. No vacations. Inflexibility. Greater and greater gaps between meaningful times in God's Word. Precious few (if any) moments in prayer and prolonged meditation.

My friend, it's time to declare it: No way can you keep going at this pace and stay effective year after year. You are H-U-M-A-N—nothing more. So, slow down! Give yourself a break! Stop trying to cover all the bases! Allow yourself time to assess your position, and—if necessary—time to heal.

MOSES ON THE FAST TRACK

Once you've put it into neutral, crack open your Bible to Exodus 18:17–27, the revealing account of a visit Jethro made to his son-in-law Moses. Old Jethro frowned as he watched Moses dash from one person to another, one crisis to the next. From morning until night Moses swam neck deep in decisions, activities, and high-stress appointments. He must have looked very impressive—cramming down a handful of manna on the run, moving fast, meeting deadlines, solving other people's problems. If he were living today, he'd probably have a beeper strapped to one hip and a cell phone to the other.

Jethro, however, wasn't impressed. "What is this thing that you are doing for the people?" he asked. Moses responded defensively (most too-busy people do) as he attempted to justify his schedule.

But Jethro didn't buy it. He advised Moses against trying to do everything alone and reproved him with strong words: "The thing that you are doing is not good. You will surely wear out" (vv. 17–18).

In other words, he told Moses: *Call for help.*

The benefits of shifting and sharing the load? Read verses 22–23: "It will be easier for you. . . . You will be able to endure." Isn't that interesting? We seem to think it's better to wear that tired-blood, overworked-underpaid, I've-really-got-it-rough look. Among Christians, it's what I call the martyr complex: "I'm working so hard for Jesus!"

The truth is that a hurried, harried appearance usually means, "I'm too stubborn to slow down" or "I'm too insecure to say no" or "I'm too proud to ask for help." But since when is a bleeding ulcer a sign of spirituality, or a seventy-hour week a mark of efficiency?

If the world is beginning to get you down, if you find yourself too tired to pray, if you're constantly ticked off at a lot of folks—let me suggest one of the few four-letter words God loves to hear us use: HELP!

It's the first and best word to use . . . when you're starting where you are.

And just in case anyone ever tries to tell you differently, please remember this: *Life assessment and healing take time.* Stay with me for the next few pages and I'll show you what I mean.

⌒ ∞ ⌒

HELP!
It's the first and best word to use . . .
When you're starting where you are.

Chapter 2

A TIME TO HEAL

*H*ippocrates was a Greek physician considered by many to be "the Father of Medicine." It is he, you may recall, who wrote the immortal Hippocratic Oath still taken by those entering the practice of medicine.

This ancient physician lived somewhere between 450 B.C. and 375 B.C., which makes him a contemporary of other philosophical thinkers such as Socrates, Dionysius, Plato, and Aristotle.

Hippocrates wrote much more than the famous oath that bears his name. Other pieces of fine literature flowed from his pen, many of which still exist. Most of his works, as we might expect, deal with the human anatomy, medicine, and healing.

In a piece titled *Aphorisms,* for example, he wrote: "Extreme remedies are very appropriate for extreme diseases." On another occasion he authored *Precepts*. These words appear in the first chapter: "Healing is a matter of time."

While reading those thoughts recently, it occurred to me that one might connect them in a paraphrase full of significance and relevance for our own day:

Recovering from extreme difficulties usually requires an extreme amount of time.

In our microwave culture, that statement may not sound terribly encouraging. "Slow" finds little place in our accepted vocabulary. We say traffic is slow, lines are slow, or—horrors—the download time off the Internet is slow. We have very little patience for activities or enterprises that compel us to wait.

But more often than not, real recovery *is* slow. It takes time. And the deeper the wound, the more extensive the damage or trauma, the greater amount of time may be required for us to recover.

Wise counsel, Hippocrates! We tend to forget your insightful advice.

AN OLD TESTAMENT CONNECTION?

Where would the old Greek doctor get such wisdom? His *Aphorisms* and *Precepts* sound almost like the Proverbs of Solomon. As a matter of fact, the more you read his writings, the more similar to Solomon they sound.

While entertaining that thought the other day, I pondered an idea I had never before considered. Hippocrates lived sometime between Solomon the king and Paul the apostle, during the between-the-Testaments era, a four-hundred-year span of time when no Scripture was being written (although the Old Testament books were being compiled).

Here's my thought in the form of a question: Could it be that in his research the Greek philosopher came across some of Solomon's writings and rephrased a line or two? Isn't it possible that something from Solomon's journal (Ecclesiastes, by name) could have found its way into the old man's writings?

Consider the first few lines from Ecclesiastes 3:

> There is an appointed time for everything.
> And there is a time for every event under heaven—
> A time to give birth, and a time to die;
> A time to plant, and a time to uproot what is planted.
> A time to kill, and a time to heal;
> A time to tear down, and a time to build up.
> A time to weep, and a time to laugh;
> A time to mourn, and a time to dance.
>
> Ecclesiastes 3:1–4

Tucked away in that third verse is the phrase that intrigues me. *"A time to heal."* Perhaps I am only imagining all this, but I cannot help but wonder if Hippocrates' words, "Healing is a matter of time," might have found their origin in Solomon's statement. We may never know for sure. In any event, the statement remains sound, both medically and biblically. More often than not, healing truly does take time.

Recovering from extreme difficulties usually requires an extreme amount of time.

WHEN HEALING ISN'T QUICK

In thirty-eight years of ministry I have met thousands of people who hurt, their pain caused by every conceivable source. The most disillusioned among them anticipated but did not enjoy quick recovery.

Many of these hurting folks were promised a "miracle"—but when no divine intervention transpired as advertised, their anguish reached the breaking point. I have looked into their faces and heard their cries. I have witnessed their response—everything from quiet disappointment to bitter, cursing cynicism . . . from tearful sadness to violent acts of suicide. Most have been sincere, intelligent, Christian people.

Many other ministers, it seems, enjoy the role of leading people into rapid relief of pain. I could easily envy such a joyful and popular ministry. More often than not, however, it seems my lot to help those who do not "heal in a hurry"—no matter how hard they try, no matter how firmly they believe, no matter how sincerely they pray.

Even though I would love to perform instant miracles (or at least promise recovery "within a week or two"), I am not able to do so. Maybe that is the reason I am so intrigued with the combined thoughts of Hippocrates and Solomon. Since I deal constantly with people in pain, I am left to search for answers that make sense, even though they will never make headlines.

The next chapters are about the answers I have found. I have no cure-all solutions to offer, no secret formula that will get you on your feet, smiling, in twenty-four hours. I wish I did, but I don't. Yet I do have some things to say that may give you fresh hope and renewed perspective in your process of recovery.

While I cannot guarantee you healing as a result of your reading these pages, I can promise you this: a God who cares, a God whose plan is unsearchable, whose ways are unfathomable, and whose counsel is dependable. A solid grasp of God's Word will never leave you in the lurch or disillusioned, since it does not come from philosophical meanderings or superstitious hocus-pocus.

That is our starting place. And starting there, we cannot go wrong.

That is our starting place. And
starting there, we cannot go wrong.

Chapter 3

STORMY SEAS

uring our years in sunny Southern California, I saw a lot of bumper stickers that read: I'D RATHER BE SAILING. But in all those years of cruising the L.A. freeways, I don't think I ever saw one that read: I'D RATHER BE SHIPWRECKED.

I doubt that I ever will see such a sign. Sailing across the water is an exhilarating, ecstatic experience, but sinking under the water is nothing short of terrifying, especially if the sea is rough and the winds are stormy.

Movie audiences across our country watched Hollywood's re-creation of the wreck and sinking of the *Titanic* with horrified fascination. Who could watch those scenes of terror and mayhem without shuddering . . . without projecting yourself into the midst of that wild panic on that icy black night in the Atlantic?

During my hitch in the Marine Corps, I once spent over a month on the high seas. I have suffered through my share of high waves and maddening windstorms. On one occasion the swells rose somewhere between thirty and forty feet high and no one—not even the skipper—thought we would ever see land again. Talk about feeling helpless!

Enduring such life-threatening situations gives one an absolutely realistic perspective on and profound respect for the sea. I never see a large oceangoing vessel without flashing back to my days on the Pacific. How different from what I expected! Instead of an uninterrupted calm, a relaxed voyage in the buoyant waters of the deep, my whole world turned topsy-turvy. Every time I hear some novice speak glibly about how much fun it would be to sail a little boat across the seas, I shudder.

WHEN THE SAILS GO LIMP

What we expect is seldom what we experience. This came home to me in a fresh way sometime ago when I read about the twenty-year reunion of most of those who helped form the old American Football League. The seasoned sports veterans and owners swapped stories and enjoyed a full evening of laughs and reflections together.

Among those present was Al Davis, longtime owner of the Oakland Raiders. He looked at all those sitting at his table and recalled an eventful evening back in 1959 when they all stared with envy at Nicky Hilton, the scheduled speaker. On that long-ago night everyone's feelings of expectation rose another notch when Hilton was introduced as having recently made $100,000 in the baseball business in the city of Los Angeles.

Hilton stood to his feet as the place broke into thunderous applause. When he stepped to the microphone, however, he said he needed to correct the details of his introduction. It was not he who'd enjoyed that experience, but his brother Baron. And it wasn't in Los Angeles, but rather San Diego. And it wasn't baseball, but football. And it wasn't $100,000, it was $1 million. And he didn't make it, he *lost* it!

It's amazing what you discover when you look beneath the surface, isn't it? Realism almost always takes the wind out of idealism's sails.

A man named Paul certainly knew what it's like to see the winds die and the sails go limp. For years this first-century man nurtured one great dream: to visit Rome, the capital of the empire. He longed to gain an audience with Nero and, eyeball to eyeball, present to him the claims of Jesus Christ.

Realism almost always takes the wind out of idealism's sails.

Not a bad idea! Sounds like a worthy objective, a reasonable goal for an apostle of Jesus Christ. When you consider that getting to Rome called for a lengthy seagoing voyage from Palestine to Italy, you could almost envision a Mediterranean cruise. Time to rest . . . time to reflect . . . time to get some correspondence finished.

But it wasn't a cruise at all; it was a disaster. The ship didn't sail; it sank. And he didn't arrive immediately in Italy; he landed fifty miles south of Sicily. And it wasn't the splendid metropolis of Rome; it was the rugged island named Malta.

What a disappointment!

Picture in your mind the fierce storm and the panic that must have swept over those who just barely escaped with their lives:

> All of us in the ship were two hundred and seventy-six persons. And when they had eaten enough, they began to lighten the ship by throwing out the wheat into the sea. And when day came, they could not recognize the land; but they did observe a bay with a beach, and they resolved to drive the ship onto it if they could. And casting off the anchors, they left them in the sea while at the same time they were loosening the ropes of the rudders; and hoisting the foresail to the wind, they were heading for the beach. But striking a reef where two seas met, they ran the vessel aground; and the prow stuck fast and remained immovable, but the stern began to be broken up by the force of the waves. And the soldiers' plan was to kill the prisoners, that none of them should swim away and escape; but the centurion, wanting to bring Paul safely through, kept them from their intention, and commanded that those who could swim should jump overboard first and get to land, and the rest should follow, some on planks, and others on various things from the ship. And thus it happened that they all were brought safely to land. (Acts 27:37–44)

All two hundred seventy-six souls survived—a miracle in itself. They swam, gagged, gasped, struggled, then finally sloshed ashore. Safe yet soaked. Alive yet exhausted.

And they found themselves on an unexpected, tumul-tuous, time-consuming detour. All along they had Italy in their sights, the dream of Rome in their hearts . . . but now were dumped on an out-of-the-way island named Malta.

How could they not ask themselves, *What now?*

How Could They Not Ask Themselves, *What Now?*

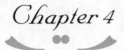

Chapter 4

WHERE RECOVERY BEGINS

*V*ictims need what places like Malta can provide. Yes, it may seem to be a barren, lonely, desperate spot, and not at all where you'd intended to be. But its therapy is solitude, and its quiet, gentle breezes bring renewal, refreshment, and healing. In a word, that's *recovery* . . . which, I remind you, takes time.

May I go a bit deeper?

It may surprise you to realize that God *plans* our Maltas. These transitional islands may seem forlorn and fearsome, especially if you arrive there on the edge of despair, suffering from a neurotic drive to accomplish more, more, more.

Those who opt for burning out en route to Rome fear rusting out at Malta. But that seldom occurs. On the contrary, it takes a Malta to show us how to stop "just existing" and start living again. What appears as nothing more than the death of a dream is, in actuality, the first step in the process of healing . . . the very essence of "starting where you are."

A FORCED BREAK

As any student of the New Testament would tell you, Paul's life over the previous twelve to fifteen months had been anything but serene. Forced to appear before several frowning judges in one courtroom after another, the apostle also had endured mob violence, physical abuse, demonic and satanic oppression, imprisonment, the pain of misunderstanding by friend and foe alike, and more than one threat on his life.

Most of those things he endured alone . . . so toss in the loneliness factor. The storm at sea seemed a fitting and climactic analogy for those long months prior to the shipwreck off the coast of Malta.

Forgive me if I sound uncaring, but it took a shipwreck to jolt Paul's perspective back into focus. The disaster at sea, followed by the forced change of pace on Malta, was precisely what he needed to begin the process of recuperation and repair.

⌐ •• ⌐

It takes a Malta to show us how to stop *just existing* and start *living* again.

For many years I have admired Sir Winston Churchill, the late prime minister of England. Through intense years of political pressure, heightened by his country's devastating war with Nazi Germany, Churchill maintained a remarkable sense of balance. His wisdom and wit remained intact, and panic never seemed to drain his inner reservoir of confident hope. I have studied his life with keen curiosity. He once wrote a brief essay titled, "Painting as a Pastime," in which he unveiled his secret of sustaining such a peaceful mind-set. It is worth our careful attention.

Many remedies are suggested for the avoidance of worry and mental overstrain by persons who, over prolonged periods, have to bear exceptional responsibilities and discharge duties upon a very large scale. Some advise exercise, and others, repose. Some counsel travel, and others retreat. Some praise solitude, and others, gaiety. No doubt all these may play their part according to the individual temperament. But the element which is constant and common in all of them is Change.

Change is the master key. A man can wear out a particular part of his mind by continually using it and tiring it, just in the same ways as he can wear out the elbows of his coat. There is, however, this difference between the living cells of the brain and inanimate articles: One cannot mend the frayed elbows by rubbing the sleeves or shoulders; but the tired parts of the mind can be rested and strengthened, not merely by rest, but by using other parts. It is not enough merely to switch off the lights which play upon the main and ordinary field of interest; a new field of interest must be illuminated.

It is no use saying to the tired mental muscles—if one may

coin such an expression—"I will give you a good rest." "I will go for a long walk," or "I will lie down and think of nothing." The mind keeps busy just the same. If it has been weighing and measuring, it goes on weighing and measuring. If it has been worrying, it goes on worrying. It is only when new cells are called into activity, when new stars become the lords of the ascendant, that relief, repose, refreshment are afforded.

A gifted American psychologist has said, "Worry is a spasm of the emotion; the mind catches hold of something and will not let it go." It is useless to argue with the mind in this condition. The stronger the will, the more futile the task. One can only gently insinuate something else into its convulsive grasp. And if this something else is rightly chosen, if it is really attended by the illumination of another field of interest, gradually, and often quite swiftly, the old undue grip relaxes and the process of recuperation and repair begins.[1]

Lest you think that "doing nothing" is the only thing involved in stopping over at Malta, reconsider Churchill's good counsel. Paul does not merely walk along the beach and finger a few seashells. Nor does he spend weeks staring at sunsets and wiggling his toes in the sand. For him to heal, he needed more than stoic silence.

He needed *change*.

Chapter 5

THE SHAPE OF CHANGE

r. Luke, the writer of Acts, mentions only a couple of the incidents that transpired between Paul and the island natives. One translation refers to these people as "rough islanders," implying that a limited education drove them to superstitious beliefs. How superstitious? That should become obvious in the account we're about to examine.

EXTRAORDINARY KINDNESS

The natives showed us extraordinary kindness; for because of the rain that had set in and because of the cold, they kindled a fire and received us all. But when Paul had gathered a bundle of sticks and laid them on the fire, a viper came out because of the heat, and fastened on his hand. And when the natives saw the creature hanging from his hand, they began saying to one another, "Undoubtedly this man is a murderer, and though he has been saved from the sea, justice has not allowed him to live." (Acts 28:2–4)

Initially, the shipwreck victims were greeted with consideration and hospitality. An early winter rainstorm drenched the island and left everyone shivering because of the cold. Responding to the disaster with admirable concern and care, the islanders built a large fire and looked after the visitors' needs.

Suddenly, however, the scene changed.

UNJUST CRITICISM

Aroused by the heat of the fire, a viper crawled out of the stack of wood and fastened itself to Paul's hand. Its fangs bit so deeply and penetratingly into the surprised apostle's flesh that at first he was unable to shake free from the snake.

The natives who observed the incident jumped to a conclusion both cruel and inaccurate. Instantly they judged that Paul's calamity proved his guilt.

Interestingly, even though these barbarians (the actual Greek term) lacked education and refined culture, they possessed an inner standard of justice. They leapt to an instantaneous (albeit incorrect) opinion: *"Undoubtedly this man is a murderer."* To them the vicious snakebite represented justice getting her due.

There is something amazingly relevant about this episode. A "punishment" mind-set is not limited to rough islanders in the Mediterranean. Heathen tribespeople aren't the only ones who jump to the erroneous conclusion that those who suffer are simply getting what they deserve. This "calamity-is-proof-of-guilt" attitude lives on with us today, a blunder as old as time itself.

The classic case in Scripture is Job. Here was an upright man who worked hard, dealt honestly with people, reared a fine family, and walked with his God. Then suddenly, seemingly out of nowhere, a whirlwind of multiple tragedies drove the man to his knees.

This "calamity-is-proof-of-guilt" attitude lives on with us today . . .

It was bad enough to lose his livestock and all other means of income, but on top of that he lost each one of his children, and finally . . . his health. With hardly a moment between these calamities to catch his breath and gain a measure of equilibrium, Job was reduced to a painful hulk of humanity, covered from head to toe with oozing skin ulcers.

Exit: compassion.

Enter: thoughtless counselors of blame.

One man after another pointed a long, bony finger into the face of the sufferer, frowning at him with condemning words and advising him to confess his guilt. In effect, each one said, "You're getting what you deserve." The confrontational dialogue contained in the ancient Book of Job is remarkably relevant. Who knows? Maybe it flashed across Paul's mind when he heard, "Undoubtedly, this man is a murderer. Justice has not allowed him to live!"

I wish there were some way for sufferers to be delivered from such unjust and unfair criticism, but I know of none. It is painful enough to endure the severe blows of life, isn't it? But when words of condemnation based on superstition and prejudice bite into us, the venom is almost more than we can bear.

INAPPROPRIATE EXALTATION

Paul, however, promptly shook off the viper and went about his business. As the serpent fell into the fire, leaving Paul free from any ill effects, the natives' eyes grew large with wonder. They waited and waited for Paul to drop dead. When he didn't, when they witnessed his resilience, "they changed their minds and began to say that he was a god."

I can't help but smile when I read of this abrupt change of opinion. First the man is a murderer; now he's a god. Talk about moving from the outhouse to the penthouse! When calamity struck, he was getting his due—punishment by death. But once recovered, he is suddenly catapulted to the superhuman realm and they are ready to worship him.

A.T. Robertson, New Testament scholar of yesteryear, recalls Paul's reverse experience many years before this Malta encounter. That one occurred in a city named Lystra, where townspeople first elevated Paul to the place of a god, Mercury, and only hours later stoned him. With seasoned wisdom, Dr. Robertson adds this biting comment, "So fickle is popular favor."[1]

It is quite possible that your situation has been intensified by a similar reversal of opinion. You once knew success. You had the respect of others. You were in demand: a competent, admired, highly honored individual who drank daily from the well of fresh praise.

But how things have changed! You now find yourself "shelved" and virtually passed by, perhaps even hated. Your world has suffered a head-on collision, and you're bloody from smashing through the windshield of reversed reputation. Those who once quoted you now criticize you. *"So fickle is popular favor."*

Full recovery, I remind you, calls for a healing that takes time—and unfortunately, it cannot occur without leaving some scars. Yet the Holy Spirit, who knows so well the contents of our hearts, can transform even scar tissue into the muscle of faith.

Yet the Holy Spirit,
who knows so well the
contents of our hearts,
can transform even
scar tissue into
the muscle of faith.

Chapter 6

THE TWO SIDES OF HEALING

*P*aul had more lessons to learn on Malta, and so do we. Luke includes a couple of vignettes from the island that instruct us even today.

Now in the neighborhood of that place were lands belonging to the leading man of the island, named Publius, who welcomed us and entertained us courteously three days. And it came about that the father of Publius was lying in bed afflicted with recurrent fever and dysentery; and Paul went in to see him and after he had prayed, he laid his hands on him and healed him. And after this had happened, the rest of the people on the island who had diseases were coming to him and getting cured. And they also honored us with many marks of respect; and when we were setting sail, they supplied us with all we needed. (Acts 28:7–10)

Take a moment to notice the repeated pronouns "us" and "we." Luke, the physician—writer of the narrative—is obviously including himself.

So what's the point? Just this. Here is an educated, well-trained medical doctor, an expert at diagnosing disease—who in this case says that "recurrent fever and dysentery" put Publius's father in bed. Dr. Luke could diagnose the ailment, but he was at a loss to bring about a cure. Not so Paul. Though the apostle was not a trained, professional physician, he did possess the supernatural, God-given ability to do what Luke could not do.

INSTANT HEALING

Wise physician that he was, Dr. Luke stood back as God worked through His servant Paul who, after praying for the aging victim, "laid his hands on him and healed him." The word translated "healed" is the Greek term *iaomai,* which usually refers to instantaneous healing. An on-the-spot miracle, if you please. Of course, Paul was not the source of such power, only the vehicle, the human instrument through whom God supernaturally worked.

I am as impressed with Dr. Luke's lack of envy as I am with the apostle Paul's spiritual gift. The physician stepped aside. Although we may be certain his medical training left him little or no room for divine miracles, his theology did! Without a moment's hesitation the professional was willing to stand back and watch God do the unusual.

By the way, that last word is worth repeating for emphasis—an on-the-spot miracle is *unusual,* an exception to the general rule. For too long people have been led to believe that virtually in every case they can "expect a miracle." And to make matters worse, when the miracle doesn't occur, they are told that something is wrong with them, they are harboring sin, they are not strong enough in their faith . . . and on and on.

This idea of "instant healing" confuses multitudes today. Sufferers are promised miracles by many alleged healers—some sincere, some naïve, some professional con artists—and when the miracle fails to materialize, great damage is done. The fallout is always tragic and occasionally irreparable.

Let's understand that there *are* times when God does indeed heal. Instantly. Miraculously. Inexplicably. But such miracles are rare—unusual exceptions to the rule—and they remind us that the One who made us certainly has the power to mend our physical bodies.

An on-the-spot miracle is *unusual,* an exception to the general rule.

PROLONGED RECOVERY

Look again at the last part of this account: "After this had happened, the rest of the people on the island who had diseases were coming to him and getting cured. And they also honored us with many marks of respect; and when we were setting sail, they supplied us with all we needed" (Acts 28:9–10).

As the word of a miracle traveled across the island, the rest of those with ailments flocked to Paul for healing. A cursory reading of the event could leave us with the impression that everyone who came received a similar miracle. Not so. The original term used by Dr. Luke to describe the people's being "cured" is altogether different from the one he used for Publius's father. The latter word is *therapeuo,* from which we get our English word, "therapy." One reputable source writes: "It might better be translated . . . were *treated.* It suggests not miraculous healings but medical treatment, probably at the hands of Luke the physician. Verses 10 and 11 suggest that this medical ministry lasted throughout the three months stay at Malta."[1]

In other words, most of the ill went through a process, a prolonged period of recovery, which lasted perhaps for three months—maybe longer. If Luke were involved with Paul, this would be one of the earliest references in all of Scripture to "overseas medical missionary" work.

Sometimes, healing is instantaneous—*iaomai* recovery. More often than not, it takes time to heal—*therapeuo* recovery, under the care and watchful eyes of a competent medical professional.

But both forms of healing are from the hand of the Great Physician!

Chapter 7

THE BENEFITS OF TAKING TIME

*W*e seldom think of the lessons to be learned or the benefits connected to prolonged recovery. We like quick turnarounds, instant changes from sickness to health. We much prefer accounts of miracles to long, non-sensational stories of slow recoveries. In fact, we tend to grow impatient with those who can't seem to take our advice and "snap out of it" or "get well soon," like the greeting card urges (pushes?) them to do.

But like it or not, more often than not, the wise words of Hippocrates are true: "Healing is a matter of time."

Respect Rather Than Resentment

The one who needs time to heal—perhaps months or even years—often becomes the recipient of resentment. Instead of being affirmed and encouraged to press on through the pain, allowing sufficient time to get better, the sufferer encounters resentment and impatience. Uninvited advice, dripping with misunderstanding and disrespect, begins to flow.

This is especially true of those who must climb out of a background of emotional trauma. It took years for the damage to be done, yet many expect overnight recovery. For some there is the added stigma of attempted suicide or time spent in a psychiatric ward or mental hospital. Others must live with a past strewn with bitter experience. Prison. Divorce. Rape. Child abuse. Ego-shattering blows to their self-esteem.

No one on the face of the earth would more love to be healed and return to the mainstream of life than these strugglers. But for them, the therapy remains a prolonged and painful process, not an instant miracle.

My plea is that we love and respect these sufferers rather than resent them. I realize some may go to the extreme, play on our sympathy, and take advantage of our compassion. But more often than not, those who are recovering want nothing more than to be well, whole, responsible, functioning adults who carry their share of the load.

Just as it is possible to hurry the very young through childhood, refusing to give them the benefit of growing up slowly and securely, so it is possible to hurry the deeply wounded through recovery, robbing them of the benefits of healing slowly and permanently.

WISDOM, NOT JUST KNOWLEDGE

While I have spent most of my time speaking to those who minister to the hurting, I have not said much to the sufferer personally. Let me speak to you for a moment.

A major benefit of taking time to heal occurs *within* you. Almost imperceptibly, you become a person with keener sensitivity, a broader base of understanding, and a longer fuse. Patience is a by-product of pain. So is tolerance of others and obedience to God. For lack of a better title, let's call the whole package "wisdom."

For too many years in your life you have operated strictly on the basis of knowledge—human absorption of facts and natural reaction to others. But affliction has now entered your life, and even though you would much prefer to have it over with, it has not ended. Difficult though it may be for you to believe, the pain you are forced to endure is reshaping and remaking you deep within. As the psalmist once wrote:

> Before I was afflicted I went astray,
> But now I keep Thy word . . .
> It is good for me that I was afflicted,
> That I may learn Thy statutes . . .
> I know, O LORD, that Thy judgments are righteous,
> And that in faithfulness Thou hast afflicted me.
>
> Psalm 119:67,71,75

A glance back over those words is worthwhile. The psalmist admits that prolonged affliction gave him a much greater desire to obey (v. 67), a much more teachable spirit (v. 71), and a much less arrogant attitude (v. 75).

Human knowledge comes naturally, is enhanced by schooling, and enlarged by travel. But with such knowledge there often comes carnal pride, a sense of self-sufficiency, and tough independence. This kind of knowledge can prompt us to become increasingly disinterested in the spiritual dimension of life. As our reservoir of horizontal knowledge grows, our skin gets thicker and often our inner being (called "the heart" in Scripture) becomes calloused.

So God opens the door to pain.

Some physical ailment or emotional collapse or period of uncertainty levels us to mere mortality. Or a domestic conflict explodes and we are reduced to a cut above zero. The affliction (whatever it may be) paralyzes our productivity and we are cast adrift in a sea of private turmoil and, possibly, public embarrassment. To make matters worse, we are convinced we'll never recover.

At just such a dead-end street, divine Wisdom waits to be embraced. She brings with her a beautiful blend of insight— the kind we never had with all our "knowledge"—genuine humility, a perception of others, and an incredible sensitivity toward God.

Without this prolonged period of recovery, such God-given wisdom may very well pass you by. During the time it takes you to heal, wisdom replaces knowledge. The vertical dimension comes into clearer focus.

During the time it takes you to heal, wisdom replaces knowledge.

BALANCE ... FREEDOM FROM EXTREMES

It's been my observation (of myself and others) that a lengthy recovery time rivets into our heads the importance of bringing our lives back from the fringes of the extreme. In other words, lengthy recoveries teach us the value of balance.

I especially have in mind either the extreme of *too much work,* where our world is too structured, too product-oriented, too intense and responsible (to the point of neurosis), or *too little work,* where irresponsibility, inactivity, and indifference have marked our paths. During the recovery stage, it is amazing how God enables us to see the foolish extremes of our former lives.

A man recovering from a stress-induced emotional breakdown has the rare opportunity to take an airplane view of his life. *When did he start pushing himself so ruthlessly? Why did he cancel vacations? Work all those weekends? How did he get stuck in that hamster wheel anyway?*

A woman facing financial ruin due to mounting credit-card debt on top of college loans, a huge mortgage, and car payments might get into the same airplane to view her own life. *When did she start placing so much value in "things"? Why hadn't she disciplined herself to put some money away? How did she get into the habit of unrestrained spending?*

As a result of such tendencies toward extremes, many people break—and the inner destruction leaves them in shambles. It takes time to reorder and balance out our personal lives.

Chapter 8

STRONG WINDS, DEEP ROOTS

There are at least two general ways in which you may respond to a chapter on this subject. First, you may find yourself encouraged and relieved because these things make sense. You agree, more often than not, that it takes time to heal. And you feel affirmed in the healing process. Perhaps you were getting anxious and jumping to some false conclusions, misreading God's silence and failing to glean His wisdom. You have decided to rest rather than strive.

I am sincerely grateful that you have "hung tough," as my kids used to say in their teens. Your determination to learn and to grow through these stretching days will be *abundantly* rewarded.

The roots grow deep when the winds are strong. Working through is always—*always*—more painful than walking out. But in the end, ah, what confident honesty, what calm assurance, what character depth result!

Second, you may still be making up your mind. Some of this sounds reasonable. You identify and agree with several of the points I have made, but you're not ready to come down with both feet and say, "Yes, that's where I stand."

You may be pleased (and surprised) to know that I consider your response quite intelligent. Who can fully comprehend the subject of pain? Working through these issues is intensely difficult, sometimes terribly complex. I can address them in these few pages, but in no way have I mastered the message I proclaim. How can anyone know how all these things fit together in God's perfect plan?

So my counsel to all is that you join me in continuing to search for answers. Let's listen to the wisdom of the Scriptures. Let's pay close attention to the "still, small voice" of God who, as C. S. Lewis expressed it, whispers to us in our pleasures and shouts to us in our pain.

As we take time to heal . . . as we seek to assess our whereabouts and consult our compass . . . let's also take time to hear, to care, to accept, to affirm, and to pray. Let's never miss the opportunity to say, "I love you. I am with you, no matter how long it takes for you to heal."

Words like these strike a match in the darkness of confusion and pain. And when that match touches a lantern called hope, the way before us becomes bright indeed.

Thank God for hope!

Who can fully comprehend
the subject of pain?

Chapter 9

A STEADY LIGHT
IN THE DISTANCE

How I cherish the childhood memory of floundering with my father! Armed with a beat-up Coleman lantern, two gigs, a stringer . . . and clothed in old sneakers, faded jeans, torn shirts, and funny hats, we'd head into the water. When the sky grew nice and dark, we'd wade in about knee-deep and stumble off into the night, ready to stab a few flat, brown creatures who had chosen our shoreline as the place for a shrimp supper.

Actually, my dad was more addicted to floundering than I. He went to get the fish. I went to be with him . . . which was fine for a while. By and by we'd round the point about a mile from the bay cottage where the other members of the Swindoll tribe had gathered. If we stopped and listened, we could hear them either singing together or laughing like crazy. And here we were—knee-deep in muddy, cold, salt water, with nothing but thick darkness in front of us. To this day I remember looking back wistfully over my shoulder toward that ever-so-tiny light in the distance.

A few steps farther and it was out of sight.

Soon I began asking myself *why*. Why in the world had I agreed to come? Why hadn't I stayed back with the family? And if I asked him once, I must have asked a dozen times, "How much longer, Daddy? When are we gonna turn around?" In tones mellow and quiet, he comforted me.

I asked, "What if the mantle burns out?"

He had a flashlight.

"What if the batteries are dead?"

He knew the path to get us back.

While he searched for flounder, I listened for those marvelous words, "Well, Son, this is far enough. Let's turn around." Instantly, I found myself wading on tiptoes, caring nothing about finding some poor flounder—only that light, that tiny signal in the distance that assured me my dad really knew the way.

Once spotted, my entire personality changed. My anxieties vanished. My questions were answered. Hope lit the darkness like a thousand lanterns . . . thanks to one tiny light at the end of my childhood tunnel of fears.

Decades have passed since I trudged through the darkness with my father, but they have not erased from my mind the incredible importance of hope. Its significance seems larger than life to me today. How powerful is its presence!

Take from us our wealth and we are hindered.

Take our health and we are handicapped.

Take away our purpose and we are slowed, temporarily confused.

But take away our hope and we are plunged into deepest darkness . . . stopped dead in our tracks, paralyzed. Wondering, *Why?* Asking, "How much longer? Will this darkness ever end? Does He know where I am?"

How sweet it is when the Father says, "That's far enough!" Like blossoms in the snow, long-awaited color returns to our life. The stream, once frozen, starts to thaw. Hope revives and washes over us.

Inevitably, spring follows winter. Every year. Yes, including this one. Barren days, like naked limbs, will soon be clothed with fresh life.

Do you need that reminder today? Are you ready for some sunshine on your shoulders . . . a few green sprouts poking up through all that white? A light at the end of your tunnel?

Look! There it is in the distance. It may be tiny, but it's there. You made it! Your Father knew exactly where He was going. And why. And for how long. That cottage in the distance? Let's name it New Hope. You'll soon be there, laughing and singing again with the family. There is nothing like light, however small and distant, to put us on tiptoes in the darkness.

Believe it or not, you may live to see the day when your journey into darkness can be named among your most cherished memories.

Part Two
Lift Your Gaze:

~ •• ~

Beginning Your
Journey toward Leadership

Once you know where you are, you need to know where you are going. Once you have allowed the time for recovery and healing, you need to look out toward the horizon and determine what it is you must do. To accomplish such a life transition, you need to grasp the elements of leadership.

In our overpopulated, impersonal world, it is easy to underestimate the significance of one such leader . . . one leader like you.

With so many people, most of whom seem so much more capable, more gifted, more prosperous, more important than I, who am I to think my part amounts to much?

That's the way folks think. They really do. Maybe you've found yourself stuck in that mental trough too.

Aren't you glad Patrick Henry didn't occupy such a rut?

And Henry Ford? And Martin Luther King Jr.? And General Norman Schwarzkopf? And Martin Luther? And Winston Churchill? And Jackie Robinson? And Abraham Lincoln? And Mother Teresa? And Margaret Thatcher?

Ah, but it's a different world today, man. Back then, there was room for an individual to emerge and stand out in a crowd. You can't do that anymore.

Wrong! God has always underscored individual involvement. He still does.

How many did it take to help the victim who got mugged on the Jericho road? *One good Samaritan.* (More about that later!)

How many were chosen by God to confront Pharaoh and lead the Exodus? *One.*

How many sheep got lost and became the object of concern to the shepherd? *One.*

How many were needed to confront adulterous David and bring him to his knees in full repentance? *One.*

How many prophets were called to stand before the wicked King Ahab and predict drought? *One.*

How many did the Lord use to get the attention of the land of Palestine and prepare the way for Messiah? *One.*

Never, *never* underestimate the power of one.

Never, *never* underestimate the power of
ONE.

Many centuries ago, a woman almost did. She thought things were too far gone. And she certainly didn't think there was anything she could do. It was only a matter of time before all the Jews would be exterminated. Her name was Esther, and she was the Jewish wife of a Persian king, a man who was about to be tricked into making an irrevocable, disastrous decision. All Jews would be exterminated.

But the tide could be turned by . . . guess how many? You're right. One.

In this case, one frightened but determined lady.

Esther's adoptive father, realizing that she alone held the key to her husband's heart, appealed to her conscience. "If you remain silent at this time . . . you and your father's house will perish" (Esther 4:14).

She listened to his impassioned plea. What ultimately got her attention was his final line: "And who knows whether you have not attained royalty for such a time as this?" (4:14).

That did it. She broke longstanding protocol, risked the king's deadly wrath, marched into the throne room, and spoke her heart. The result? The Jews were rescued from holocaust. One woman—only one voice—saved an entire nation.

As is true of every person who stands in the gap, she was willing to get personally involved, to the point of great sacrifice. Or, as she said, "If I perish, I perish" (4:16).

She didn't think, *Someone else should be doing this, not me.* Nor did she ignore the need because of the risk. Sacrifice! It's the stuff of which leaders—people who want to make a difference—are made.

And before you allow yourself to toss this aside, thinking, *Aw, that's for somebody else—how much difference can I make?* go

back and review the value of one. Here is how poet Edward
Everett Hale put it:

> I am one.
> But still I am one.
> I cannot do everything.
> But I can do something.
> And because I cannot do everything,
> I will not refuse to do the something that I can do.[1]

Having done that, please put aside all excuses and say to
your Lord, "What should I be doing? And where? And when?
I am Your servant."

The Lord has been waiting to hear those words from your
lips. And count on this, friend. His plan is already in place.

Please put aside all excuses and say to
your Lord,
"What should I be doing?
And where?
And when?

I am Your Servant."

Chapter 10

THE ESSENTIAL ELEMENT

Leadership is not optional;
It is essential.

eadership is not optional; it is essential. Essential for motivation and direction. Essential for evaluation and accomplishment. It is the one ingredient essential for the success of any institution or organization.

Take away leadership and it isn't long before confusion replaces vision. Students, volunteers, or employees who once dedicated themselves to their tasks begin to drift. Morale erodes. Enthusiasm fades. Cynicism poisons the atmosphere. And finally . . . the whole operation grinds to a halt.

Peter Drucker's famous line is both timeless and true: "If an enterprise fails to perform, we rightly hire, not different workers, but a new president."[1]

When there's trouble brewing at the bottom, odds are better than even that a major part of the problem is at the top. Whether the scene is business, industry, labor, government, education, athletics, military, religion, or domestic, the hope and progress of the organization rests in the hands of those who are in charge.

Realizing the essential nature of leadership, and with numerous opportunities to witness both positive and negative examples of it, I recently found myself surprised to find so little actually written on the subject—from a *biblical* point of view.

Yes, there are countless volumes on motivation and time management. How-to-do-it books on self-esteem, assertiveness, and reaching one's full potential fill shelf after shelf at bookstores. But I find very few books that take the reader to the Scriptures and allow God's Word to speak on the subject. And as you will see, the Bible has a great deal to say about leadership. Its counsel, as on every other essential life topic, is both reliable and practical.

To me, biblical counsel on leadership is anything but theoretical. For many years, I was the pastor of a local church with a multiple staff. Concurrent with those responsibilities, I served as president of an international radio ministry. Today, I am privileged to serve as president of a seminary.

The insights I will share in this chapter are being hammered out on the anvil of hands-on involvement with many people. While the major part of my work is in the religious realm, it is certainly not limited to that. For that reason, I can assure you that the ideas and principles I present are neither exclusive to the Christian who is in ministry, nor are they in any sense of the word idealistic or irrelevant.

If you find yourself on the threshold of a new phase or new venture in your life—whether that involves graduation, marriage, parenting, new career, or new responsibilities, I can heartily recommend these pages to you.

If something I write triggers a new idea or opens a door of hope, prompting fresh excitement or motivation that results in your becoming a better leader—in whatever your situation or opportunity—I will be pleased. But I am really unable to take any of the credit. All I have done is go back to an infallible source that has never failed to give sound advice. That's why I decided over thirty-eight years ago to devote myself to a lifetime study of the Scriptures. What leadership is to an organization, the Bible is to me.

It isn't optional; it's essential.

Chapter 11

THE INCREDIBLE
VALUE OF LEADERSHIP

During the prosperous sixties, Dunn and Bradstreet reported an average of more than 13,000 business failures annually. Natural and professional curiosity led them to search out why. Their analysis revealed that the lion's share of these casualties (approximately 92 percent) were due to managerial difficulties.

In a word, leadership.

The facts don't lie—businesses and institutions don't fail until the leaders do.

Who hasn't gone into a restaurant once noted for its splendid reputation, only to be disappointed. Instead of an elegant, enjoyable setting, the place looked run-down. Unkempt. You expected superb service and delectable food placed before you in a creative and first-class manner, but both server and cuisine let you down. As an astute observer, you realized the problem wasn't simply an irresponsible maintenance crew or a preoccupied waiter or an amateur cook . . . it was management.

Sometimes you can sense it in a place—be it a fine restaurant or the corner fast-food joint—as soon as you step through the door. You say to yourself, *This place is well managed!* or *This place needs a new manager!*

Who hasn't watched a favorite professional football team tumble from the top of the league to the bottom? Once a powerhouse of strength, innovation, and top-caliber players, the team now embarrasses its fans as one losing season follows another. The primary need is not another split end or a better linebacker or a bigger nose guard. Owners and players alike will agree that they need another coach. In some cases, another owner!

Decades ago, when the Chrysler Corporation decided to get serious about solving its decline in the American automobile industry, it did not change the body style on its new cars or ask its dealers across the country to paint their buildings another color. No, Chrysler hired a new and innovative leader—Lee Iacocca. And in just a few years, his name became as famous as that of his former boss, Henry Ford. To this day, the company—though now an international conglomerate—remains innovative and strong.

I experienced something similar during my years in the Marine Corps. Within a brief span of time, I watched the morale of a battalion or a company completely reverse itself. The reason? A new commander took charge.

I have seen churches, once devastated by splits or scandals, turn the corner and reach new heights in their ministry as the right leadership was chosen and given the reins of responsibility.

I have seen whole towns or cities shake off reputations for being crime-ridden and dangerous (or for being dirty and lacking self-respect) once they put into office civic leaders with a high degree of integrity, determination, and courage.

And how could anyone deny the value of leadership within a home? (You can sometimes sense *that* as soon as you walk through the front door too.) Parents or guardians who are loving, affirming, fair, and consistent in their discipline, and secure and confident in their relationship with their children—my, what a difference in that family!

How could anyone deny the value of leadership within a home?

Chapter 12

INSPIRING INFLUENCE

*L*eadership, while easy to describe, is much more difficult to define. It's much easier to recount what leaders *do* than to describe what they *are*. Good leadership is, more often than not, elusive. We know it when we see it, yet we have a tough time identifying or capsulizing the concept.

At the risk of oversimplifying, I'm going to resist a long, drawn-out definition and settle on one word. It's the word *influence*. If you will allow me two words, *inspiring influence*.

Those who do the best job of management—those most successful as leaders—use their influence to inspire others to follow, to work harder . . . to sacrifice, if necessary. Elusive though it may be, such inspiring influence generates incredible results.

- When a team finds leadership in the coach, it is remarkable how the players will strive for and achieve almost impossible feats to win.

- When a teacher has leadership abilities, the cooperation and accomplishments of the class border on the astounding.

- When a sales force finds leadership in their manager, they will knock themselves out to reach their quotas month in, month out.

This is a good time to clarify something, lest you find yourself saying, "Well, I'm just not the leadership type. I don't fit the persona." It is a false impression that all leaders must have the same temperament. Some are hard-charging types, whose style is bold, loud, and strong. But others, equally effective, may be much quieter. They seldom lift their voices above a conversational level.

I know leaders who employ extrinsic methods of motivation with a great degree of success. But I'm also acquainted with those who loathe that approach. They would much rather motivate the inner person with intrinsic appeals. There are leaders who remain aloof, while others roll up their sleeves and get personally involved with those they lead. Some leaders are highly intelligent, widely read, and scholarly in their approach. Others are not as bright intellectually, but they are seasoned, wise, and resourceful—and just as respected as their brilliant counterparts.

⌒ •• ⌒

The leader whose influence proves
most effective is the one who
gets along well with people.

Obviously, a leader's temperament (some may call it "style") will differ from one personality to the next. However leadership style may be expressed, those who respond with cooperation and commitment do so because of the inspiring influence that leader demonstrates.

Regardless of temperament, the leader whose influence proves most effective is the one who gets along well with people. The great American entrepreneur, John D. Rockefeller, once admitted, "I will pay more for the ability to deal with people than any other ability under the sun."[1]

The value of this single quality can hardly be exaggerated. According to a report by the American Management Association, an overwhelming majority of the two hundred managers who participated in the survey agreed that the single most valuable ingredient—the "paramount skill"—was the ability to get along with people. Managers rated this ability above intelligence, decisiveness, job knowledge, or technical skills.[2]

Before moving on to an outstanding biblical example, I want to add a comment to those involved in vocational Christian service. All too often (especially among those getting started in ministry), the importance of getting along well with people is downplayed. It is falsely assumed that people will automatically respect and follow one's leadership simply because of a mutual commitment to the same Lord or a mutual agreement to the same doctrine—regardless of the leader's ability to deal with people.

That is an unhappy delusion!

Time and again I have spoken with disillusioned individuals who began their service for the King with that mentality. Although they were called, schooled, dedicated, excited about their future, and faced with a choice opportunity to lead a group of people, they ultimately found themselves forced to admit that the one ingredient they thought could be overlooked was the very one they could not do without. How often I have heard the words, "If only. . . "

So then, let's expand our definition to include these all-important characteristics. Effective leaders are those whose inspiring influence prompts others to follow. While their style, level of intelligence, method of motivation, and personal involvement with the tasks may differ widely, those people who are most successful possess the same trait—the ability to get along well with others.

Chapter 13

A BIBLICAL MODEL

$\mathcal{W}$hile digging my way through one of the New Testament letters sometime ago, I happened upon a section of Scripture that spoke with remarkable relevance on the subject of leadership.

The apostle Paul sent his first letter to a small but capable band of Christians living in the bustling, wealthy metropolis of Thessalonica. Today, it's the Grecial city of Thessalonike (or Salonika), second only to Athens in size.

Like many in our busy American cities, the Thessalonians were living in the fast lane (an ancient freeway—named *Via Ignatia*—ran alongside the city) and were active citizens of a colorful and aggressive culture. Merchants, businessmen and career women, artists and laborers, philosophers and teachers comprised that small Christian community. Many of them could remember the day when they first heard the Jewish traveler from Tarsus as he spoke so courageously, so convincingly, of his conversion and of their need to believe in the Lord Jesus Christ. How could they resist?

As a sufficient number of them responded, the little church in Macedonia (northern Greece) was born; and after a few short weeks, almost as quickly as he arrived, Paul departed. His entire stay lasted no longer than two months, probably less. His travels took him on through Athens to Corinth, from where he wrote this first letter to his friends in Thessalonica.

About a year had passed. Who knows precisely what thought prompted Paul to pick up his pen and begin to write? Concerns? Curiosity? Nostalgia? Some traveler's comment received one night in Corinth? Perhaps a mixture of all the above.

The missionary began to muse. He retraced his steps and relived the excitement of those weeks he had invested in Macedonia. What eventful days! What a great group of believers!

He spoke so courageously,
so convincingly, of his conversion
and of their need to believe in
the Lord Jesus Christ.

How Could They Resist?

INITIAL FEELINGS

Just imagine the man's emotions as he wrote: "For you yourselves know, brethren, that our coming to you was not in vain, but after we had already suffered and been mistreated in Philippi, as you know, we had the boldness in our God to speak to you the gospel of God amid much opposition" (1 Thessalonians 2:1–2).

How many of us would love to look back over our shoulder someday and say, "Now *that* was not in vain!" All those hours and days and months that Paul had invested among the Thessalonians were purposeful, not empty, not hollow. Much was accomplished. It was worth the effort. Lives were changed. Decisions that relate to eternity were made. *"Not in vain!"*

Then, almost as if struck with a spasm of grief, Paul adds a comment about the pain he endured prior to his arrival. He mentions how fractured he felt when he stumbled into their city. Philippi, his previous place of ministry, had been no friend of grace to help him go on to God. There had been shameful mistreatment. "Outrageous" would say it better and be more in keeping with Paul's actual choice of terms.

While in that city he and his companion, Silas, has been beaten with rods and dumped into prison. We Christians love to talk about how miraculously they were later delivered from that awful place. But we seldom linger over the humiliation—the inhuman treatment—they endured prior to their glorious deliverance. Although torn in body, the missionary did not hesitate to speak boldly of the good news of Messiah immediately upon arriving at Thessalonica. But even that was "amid much opposition," please remember.

What's the point of all this? you may wonder. *I thought we were dealing with effective leadership; we covered pain and suffering in the last chapter.* Ironically these three elements are often inseparable. Strong leadership grows out of times of great stress and challenge. It shines forth unexpectedly, like a searchlight cutting through the fog.

Far too many today live in a dream world when it comes to preparation for leadership. There is this popular yet mistaken notion that leaders somehow emerge on the scene having been dropped from a lacy cloud—all white, ideal, and spotless—like a living Mr. Clean, "untouched by human hands." Perhaps that is the reason God led Paul to go back to those painful days when many would have said, "Now, that was in vain."

But it wasn't.

What a perfect place to begin when building a biblical model of leadership . . . the pain of mistreatment, the humiliation and loneliness of being imprisoned.

Some (dare I say most?) of God's choicest leaders have emerged from wombs of woe. The Ghetto. A prison. Shame or sickness. A broken home. Mistreatment and fear. But resiliently and triumphantly they came through. From a stormy and tumultuous world of outward opposition or personal insecurity or emotional breakdown or financial failure or physical affliction, they stand today as living trophies of grace.

⌐ •• ⌐

Strong leadership grows out of times of great stress and challenge.

My point? Disabilities need not disqualify. On the contrary, struggling makes a great background for leadership! Not unless you have struggled with the hopelessness and brokenness of life's pains can you possibly know how to lead others through such valleys. Since the prime function of the leader is to keep hope alive, its absence helps the leader never to forget its value. Yesterday's pain prompts today's praise.

It was just such thoughts that caused Aleksandr Solzhenitsyn to write: "It was only when I lay there on rotting prison straw that I sensed within myself the first stirrings of good. Gradually, it was disclosed to me that the line separating good and evil passes, not through states, nor between classes, nor between political parties either, but right through every human heart, and through all human hearts. So bless you, prison, for having been in my life."[1]

Chapter 14

FOUR APPROACHES
TO AVOID

*O*nce Paul began to reflect upon his not-in-vain visit among the Thessalonians, he opened a floodgate of memories. Living almost twenty centuries removed from those days, we have difficulty imagining how the man could have continued on despite the difficulties he encountered.

Furthermore, what characterized his leadership? How could he have been so bold? When the Thessalonians remembered him, what mental images did they entertain? All these questions and so many more are answered in the section following these opening lines we have just relived.

Paul mentions several things that did not characterize his leadership before presenting the things that did. Let's observe the negatives before considering the positives. There are four of each.

DECEPTION

> For our exhortation does not come from error or impu-
> rity or by way of deceit. (1 Thessalonians 2:3)

The self-portrait Paul paints is one of absolute honesty and sincerity. Not double-tongued, guilty of a hidden agenda or improper motives, he claims to be free from deception.

Great place to start! And all the more important since the leader has clout. A built-in role of authority exists just by virtue of the position he or she holds. Except for a few who view any and all leaders with a suspicious eye, most folks trust and hold their leader in high regard—making the role of leader a tempting target for deception by those who lack integrity.

Decades ago Elton Trueblood wrote like a prophet far ahead of his time: "It is hard to think of any job in which the moral element is lacking. The skill of the dentist is wholly irrelevant if he is unprincipled and irresponsible. There is little, in that case, to keep him from extracting teeth unnecessarily, because the patient is in a helpless situation. It is easy to see the harm that can be done by an unprincipled lawyer. Indeed, such a man is far more dangerous if he is skilled than if he is not skilled."[1]

I frequently quote to myself the statement made by Asaph, who wrote eloquently of David the king. After his masterful treatise on the early history of the Hebrew people in Psalm 78, he reserved the final three verses for David, almost like a climactic benediction:

> He also chose David His servant,
> And took him from the sheepfolds;

From the care of the ewes with suckling lambs

He brought him,

To shepherd Jacob His people,

And Israel His inheritance.

So he shepherded them according to

the integrity of his heart,

And guided them with his skillful hands.

Psalm 78:70–72

Leaders with power and brains are common. So are leaders with riches and popularity. But a competent leader full of integrity and skill, coupled with sincerity, is rare indeed.

Deception creates suspicion. Once the leader's followers begin to suspect motives or find that what is said publicly is denied privately, the thin wire of respect that holds everything in place snaps. Confidence drains away.

The late President Dwight Eisenhower stated his opinion with dogmatism: "The supreme quality for a leader is unquestionably integrity. Without it, no real success is possible, no matter whether it is a section gang, on a football field, in an army, or in an office. If his associates find him guilty of phoniness, if they find that he lacks forthright integrity, he will fail. His teachings and actions must square with each other. The first great need, therefore, is integrity and high purpose."[2]

FLATTERY

But just as we have been approved by God to be entrusted with the gospel, so we speak, not as pleasing men but God, who examines our hearts. For we never came with flattering speech, as you know. (1 Thessalonians 2:4–5)

Paul made this statement referring to the gospel he preached, but I believe it has broader application in the realm of leadership. This tendency toward flattery may be especially difficult if you are good at working with people! There is a fine but very definite line between being a leader who gets along well with people and being one who must please people (at all costs).

Few characteristics reveal one's insecurity more than this. And talk about losing respect! Not only do others fail to respect the people-pleaser, he doesn't even respect himself. By fence-sitting, by hedging the truth and attempting to keep peace at any price (a virtual impossibility), the leader forfeits the right to lead and becomes, as a consequence, a follower who still tries to call himself a leader.

I can think of few ingredients more foundational to being a good leader than knowing oneself—and accepting oneself—and feeling secure about oneself inside one's own skin. The scene is nothing short of tragic when an insecure person is given a leadership responsibility. One of the earliest signs is the very point Paul makes—flattery gets substituted for decisiveness.

Allow me this direct question: Do you know yourself? And

～ •• ～

Do you know yourself?

Do You Like Yourself?

one more: Do you *like* yourself? These basic stones must be in place, or no superstructure of meaningful accomplishment can be erected.

If you have hopes of raising your gaze toward leadership, let me urge you to start here. It may take great effort to gain a secure sense of self-esteem. It may involve pain. But in the long haul, you will be grateful you paid the price. Not until you enjoy peace with yourself, not until you know and like the things that make you what you are, will you be able to conquer the need to flatter.

In her splendid work, *Gift from the Sea,* Anne Morrow Lindbergh states her credo. Her words well up with a sense of personal security.

I want, first of all . . . to be at peace with myself. I want a single-ness of eye, a purity of intention, a central core to my life that will enable me to carry out these obligations and activities as well as I can.

I want, in fact—to borrow from the language of the saints—to live "in grace" as much of the time as possible. I am not using this term in a strictly theological sense. By grace I mean an inner harmony, essentially spiritual, which can be translated into outward harmony. I am seeking perhaps what Socrates asked for in the prayer from the Phaedrus when he said, "May the outward and the inward man be one." I would like to achieve a state of inner spiritual grace from which I could function and give as I was meant to in the eye of God.[3]

Maybe it will help to look back at a statement Paul made to the Thessalonians. We Christians have been "approved by

God," and therefore He alone "examines our hearts." It seems to me that He holds much of the secret to overcoming this insecure tendency to be a people-pleaser.

There was a time in my ministry, many years ago, when a single verse of Scripture jolted me back to a place of confidence, delivering me from the trap of telling a group of influential people what they wanted to hear. I realize now it was a turning point in my leadership pilgrimage from "slave to others" to "servant of Christ." It reads, "For am I now seeking the favor of men, or of God? Or am I striving to please men? If I were still trying to please men, I would not be a bond-servant of Christ" (Galatians 1:10).

A leader who wants to be respected can afford flattery no more than he can deception. As someone once said, "I don't know the secret of success, but I do know the secret of failure— try to please everybody!"

No successful leader maintains the respect of others without making decisions that inevitably prove unpopular.

I don't know the secret of success, but I do know the secret of failure—

Try to please everybody!

GREED

> For we never came with flattering speech, as you know, nor
> with a pretext for greed—God is witness. (1 Thessalonians 2:5)

Interestingly, Paul tells his readers that they themselves could testify that he did not speak with flattering speech ("as you know"). When it came to his refusal to conduct his life according to greed, however, he declared, "God is witness."

Anyone can see when a leader is a people-pleaser. It's no secret. It's public knowledge. But greed can be hidden, masked from public view. Yet the One who examines hearts knows the whole truth.

What a motivational cancer is greed! It's not simply the longing to get more, but the passion to possess more than one ought to possess. Greed doesn't stop with healthy and necessary competition; it strives to have the most at any cost. With wicked determination, this ruthless beast scratches and claws its way to the top, snarling defiantly and devouring whatever and whomever gets in its way.

Earlier I mentioned Lee Iacocca, a dynamo and former leader at both Chrysler and Ford Motor Company. Years ago, while reading the autobiography of this hard-boiled entrepreneur, I remember being interested to discover his feelings about greed.

After being fired by Ford, Iacocca was forced to rethink his motives and answer some gut-level questions regarding his reasons for hanging on so tenaciously at Ford. He didn't try to hide his addiction to greed. Face it, it would be tough for almost anyone to turn his back on a million a year, plus perks!

A guy with white-coated waiters available at the snap of his fingers and a chauffeur to and from work finds it extremely difficult to put on the brakes. In a moment of honesty and vulnerability, Iacocca admitted that of the seven deadly sins, greed is by far the worst. Hear him as he quotes his Italian-born father: "My father always said, 'Be careful about money. When you have five thousand, you'll want ten. And when you have ten, you'll want twenty.' He was right. No matter what you have, it's never enough."[4]

The path of many a leader is strewn with the litter of greed. Like the remora, those little shark suckers that swim alongside and attach themselves to the great predators of the sea, greed always hovers near those in leadership. The more influential the leader, the more the temptation to yield.

And don't be so naïve as to think this sort of greed is limited to those in the marketplace. Greed is just as aggressive in Christian ministry! Greed for larger crowds, more impressive results, bigger buildings—even greed for fame among one's own circles.

❧ •• ❧

The path of many a leader is strewn with the litter of greed.

Greed has three facets: love of things, love of fame, and love of pleasure; and these can be attacked directly with frugality, anonymity, and moderation. Reduction of greed will be translated into stepped-up vitality, diminished self-centeredness, and a clearer awareness of our real identity. For a permanent commitment to working with the tools of the spiritual life provides a disciplined basis for liberation from greed's tentacles.[5]

Not a bad set of priorities to pursue! Especially if you sense that your desire for more, more, more is already beginning to take its toll.

Authoritarianism

For we never came with flattering speech, as you know, nor with a pretext for greed—God is witness—nor did we seek glory from men, either from you or from others, even though as apostles of Christ we might have asserted our authority. (1 Thessalonians 2:5–6)

Because we do not live in the first century, we have trouble appreciating Paul's comment regarding his role as an "apostle of Christ." There was no higher title in the church, no more powerful or influential position than apostleship. Authentic apostolic authority accompanied him wherever he went, whatever he did, whenever he spoke. Everybody knew that when an apostle spoke, *you had better listen!*

Honestly now, wouldn't it have been tempting to massage that image just a little? Wouldn't it have been oh-so-easy to flaunt that power a bit? Or at least milk it a little to impress folks? Paul could certainly have done that. He could certainly have made himself a little Caesar of the church, demanding and receiving bows and adulation.

But he didn't. The only marks of authority he wore were his scars.

Paul refused to assert his authority, even though (as he admitted) he had every right to do so. When others attempted to glorify him, he rejected the attempt. When Christians invited him to ascend to the pedestal, he declined. When special treatment was offered to him, Paul turned it down. As a matter of fact, in his next letter to the Thessalonians, we read that he carried his share of the financial responsibilities, lest he appear as a freeloader:

> For you yourselves know how you ought to follow our example, because we did not act in an undisciplined manner among you, nor did we eat anyone's bread without paying for it, but with labor and hardship we kept working night and day so that we might not be a burden to any of you; not because we do not have the right to this, but in order to offer ourselves as a model for you, that you might follow our example. For even when we were with you, we used to give you this order: if anyone will not work, neither let him eat. (2 Thessalonians 3:7–10)

⌣ •• ⌣

What a motivational cancer is GREED.

Leaders—especially those with vast influence—frequently fall into the trap of throwing their weight around and expecting kid-glove treatment. (I heard of one nationally known pastor who demanded to be picked up at the airport for his speaking engagements in a Cadillac El Dorado. Nothing else would do.)

How unusual, yet how encouraging, to find true humility and a servant's heart among those who wield a lot of clout! Too many use their leadership status to bully or take advantage of those they lead, in the mistaken belief that their influential role justifies their prima-donna style. Where authoritarian leaders play out their self-aggrandizing goals and objectives, people become little more than pawns on a chessboard.

Michael Macoby of Harvard University, author of *The Gamesmen,* vividly portrays such persons like this: "The leader who plays games with ideas and objectives, resources, and with people . . . plays at leadership; he gets his "kicks" out of making things work. His main concern: that he is successful . . . as long as he can hang one more trophy over the fireplace of recognition, as long as he is properly remunerated."[6]

Picking up on this idea, Gordon MacDonald adds this insightful and penetrating reminder:

> The gamesman is not an alien within the Christian community. One can see traces of gamesmanship entangling vast areas of Christian activity. It is an insidious influence that leads Christians to measure the work of God in terms of numbers, square footage, and popular acceptance. . . .
>
> Today the theme that overrides any other is that of me first in blessing; me first in the feel-good experience of certain spiritual gifts; me first in terms of material comfort and

rewards. . . . The bottom line of the contemporary gospel—the one that does not produce servants—seems to be "grab the crown; avoid the cross!"[7]

So then, if you wish to pursue a brand of leadership that squares with Scripture, you must avoid these four special temptations of leadership:

> *Deception*
>   *Flattery*
>   *Greed*
>   *Authoritarianism*

So much for the negatives! Brighter, better qualities await us.

Chapter 15

FOUR APPROACHES
TO EMBRACE

For the next few pages, let's concentrate on four positive traits of effective leadership. Each one emerges like gold nuggets in a pile of river rock, flashing in the sunlight.

SENSITIVITY TO NEEDS

But we proved to be gentle among you, as a nursing mother tenderly cares for her own children. (1 Thessalonians 2:7)

Still reflecting on his days among the Thessalonians, which were "not in vain," Paul gets a bit misty. Far from the aloof, macho image of a corporate leader, the apostle compares himself to a nursing mom—a woman who graciously and unselfishly cares for the needs of her own children. Without hesitation he uses terms such as "gentleness" and "tenderness" to describe his approach—words seldom associated with strong leaders who get the job done.

But this statement brings me back to an earlier remark I made about getting along well with others. Leaders who do the best job are those whose antennae are keenly attuned to others.

They sense the scene.

They get the picture.

They read between the lines.

And having done so, they operate from a sensitive vantage point that weaves wisdom and understanding into the fabric of their leadership. People respond to such leaders with delight, because they realize their leader truly cares—cares about them personally. These leaders refuse to check folks off like so many items on a long agenda.

To carry this out, the leader must guard against a major enemy—preoccupation. He must force himself to do more than merely see; he must gain *insight*. He must do more than simply hear; he must *perceive*. The most effective leaders have the uncanny ability to spot what isn't said, to detect attitudes behind actions, facial expressions surrounding spoken words.

> Leaders who do the best job
> are those whose antennae
> are keenly attuned to others.

I laughed out loud when I read Dr. James Dobson's account of a physician whose preoccupation reached the extreme. With tongue in cheek, the good doctor writes:

> I know of a gynecologist who is not only deaf, but blind as well. He telephoned a friend of mine who is also a physician in the practice of obstetrics and gynecology. He asked for a favor.
>
> "My wife has been having some abdominal discomfort this afternoon," he said. "I don't want to treat my own wife and wonder if you'd see her for me?"
>
> My friend invited the doctor to bring his wife for an examination, whereupon he discovered (are you ready for this?) that she was five months pregnant! Her obstetrician husband was so busy caring for other patients that he hadn't even noticed his wife's burgeoning pregnancy. I must admit wondering how in the world this woman ever got his attention long enough to conceive![1]

AFFECTION FOR PEOPLE

Having thus a fond affection for you, we were well-pleased to impart to you not only the gospel of God but also our own lives, because you had become very dear to us. (1 Thessalonians 2:8).

Once again we are surprised to read that such things as love and a warm, affectionate relationship are important ingredients in effective leadership.

But indeed they are!

Even one as disciplined and determined as Paul considered

feelings of "fond affection" invaluable. Why? Because the men and women he led became "very dear" to him.

Even though Paul was tough enough to do pioneer work and brilliant enough to refine his theology in the crucible of physical abuse and emotional trauma, his genuine affection for people came through loud and clear. Whether young or old, famous or obscure, healthy or sickly, sharp or dull, people who got close to the great apostle felt loved . . . because they *were* loved.

AUTHENTICITY OF LIFE

Nor did we eat anyone's bread without paying for it, but with labor and hardship we kept working night and day so that we might not be a burden to any of you; not because we do not have the right to this, but in order to offer ourselves as a model for you, so that you might follow our example.
(2 Thessalonians 3:8–9)

⌣

A leader who loves people must some-how demonstrate that.

This Requires Authenticity.

A leader who loves people must somehow *demonstrate* that. This requires authenticity—and even a measure of transparency.

Did you catch what Paul said about his personal style? I don't want us to miss it, since it's a major secret of good leadership. He was pleased to impart "not only the gospel," but also his *"own life."* With that kind of leader, you don't have to settle for a truckload of truth dumped into your ears, and nothing more. You also got, along with the truth, authentic reality—his own life. The man had nothing to hide.

Paul goes on to say he worked among them, and in doing so, he behaved "uprightly and blamelessly."

In other words, he practiced what he preached.

Is it any wonder God was so pleased to use this leader to such a remarkable extent? No pompous air about him. No distant, demanding despot who came, saw, and conquered. No visiting lecturer who remained aloof and lived in a world of touch me-not secrecy. On the contrary, he was approachable, accessible, a leader who loved, whom people could get next to, whom God would use to shape the early history of His church.

It was not unusual for Paul to be this open. Time and again in his letters, he combined authenticity with affection. For example, consider similar words addressed to the Corinthians:

In the same way, my brothers, when I came to proclaim to you God's secret purpose, I did not come equipped with any brilliance of speech or intellect. You may as well know now that it was my secret determination to concentrate entirely on Jesus Christ himself and the fact of his death upon the cross. As a matter of fact, in myself I was feeling far from strong; I was nervous and rather shaky. What I said and preached had none of the attractiveness of the clever mind, but it was a demonstration of the power of the Spirit! Plainly God's purpose was that your faith should rest not upon man's cleverness but upon the power of God. (1 Corinthians 2:1–5, PHILLIPS)

Paul wrote openly of his trials and struggles ("conflicts without, fears within"). He considered none of that his own private world. While he refused to play on others' emotions to manipulate them, he insisted on remaining vulnerable and unguarded when it came to his own humanity . . . as when he wrote his friends in Philippi:

It has been a great joy to me that after all this time you have shown such renewed interest in my welfare. I don't mean that you had forgotten me, but up till now you had no opportunity of expressing your concern. Nor do I mean that I have been in actual need, for I have learned to be content, whatever the circumstances may be. I know now how to live when things are difficult and I know how to live when things are prosperous. In general and in particular I have learned the secret of facing either plenty or poverty. I am ready for anything through the strength of the one who lives within me. Nevertheless I am not disparaging the way in which you were willing to share my troubles. You Philippians will remember that in the early days of the gospel when I left Macedonia, you were the only church who shared with me the fellowship of giving and receiving. Even in Thessalonica you twice sent me help when I was in need. It isn't the value of the gift that I am keen on; it is the reward that will be come to you because of these gifts that you have made.

Now I have everything I want—in fact I am rich. Yes, I am quite content, thanks to your gifts received through Epaphroditus. Your generosity is like a lovely fragrance, a sacrifice that pleases the very heart of God. (Philippians 4:10–18, PHILLIPS)

The popular yet mistaken image of a successful leader, male or female, is the aloof, tough-minded, tough-talking executive who operates in a world of untouchable, sophisticated secrecy. If he or she has needs, feels alone, wrestles with very human problems, or lacks the ability to cope with some particular pressure, no one should ever know about it. And certainly there is no place for tears! That would be an embarrassing sign of vulnerability, and no leader who swims with the sharks can ever reveal such weakness. Real leaders don't cry . . . nor do they show any other emotion except a self-assured air of confidence.

Where did we pick up such inhuman ideas? Since when is it a sign of weakness to be real . . . to admit needs . . . to show affection? And why do we have such an aversion to tears? The best leaders, the men and women in my life who have impacted me most significantly, have usually been those who allowed me into their private world, who expressed (and proved) their love for me.

Often when they were moved or hurt, they wept.

When they were unsure, they said so.

When they were disappointed, they put it out on the table.

When they struggled, they admitted it.

These leaders were strong and competent, but they were also real. One hundred percent human, with no phony Wall Street or Madison Avenue glaze coating their authentic feelings and desires. Leaders who exhibit such balance never fail to earn my respect.

On the one-hundred-fiftieth anniversary of the birthday of Abraham Lincoln, the distinguished poet and historian Carl Sandburg was invited to Washington D. C. to speak. Before a joint session of Congress and assembled diplomatic corps, the astute, eloquent student of Lincoln held the attention of everyone as he portrayed a very great leader with very human characteristics. Calling his speech, appropriately, "Man of Steel and Velvet," Sandburg helped everyone see that a respected leader can be both capable and vulnerable. The mixture may be rare, but when it exists, it is truly effective.

> Not often in the story of mankind does a man arrive on earth who is both steel and velvet, who is as hard as rock and soft as drifting fog, who holds in his heart and mind the paradox of terrible storm and peace unspeakable and perfect. . . .
>
> While the war winds howled, he insisted that the Mississippi was one river meant to belong to one country. . . .

╲ ●● ╱

These leaders were strong and competent, but they were also *Real.*

While the luck of war wavered and broke and came again, as generals failed and campaigns were lost, he held enough forces . . . together to raise new armies and supply them, until generals were found who made war as victorious war has always been made, with terror, frightfulness, destruction . . . valor and sacrifice past words of man to tell.

In the mixed shame and blame of the immense wrongs of two crashing civilizations, often with nothing to say, he said nothing, slept not at all, and on occasions he was seen to weep in a way that made weeping appropriate, decent, majestic.[2]

ENTHUSIASTIC IN AFFIRMATION

You are witnesses, and so is God, how devoutly and uprightly and blamelessly we behaved toward you believers; just as you know how we were exhorting and encouraging and imploring each one of you as a father would his own children, so that you may walk in a manner worthy of the God who calls you into His own kingdom and glory. (1 Thessalonians 2:10–12)

Did you notice those descriptive terms?

"Exhorting . . . encouraging . . . imploring?" And did you catch the analogy? "As a father would his own children." Earlier Paul wrote of the tenderness of a nursing mother. Here he mentions the enthusiastic affirmation of a father.

This is no picture of oppressive, relentless harassment, but rather one of reassuring encouragement . . . the you-can-do-it, hang-in-there confidence of a dad with his children.

My wife and I are the parents of four grown children. All four attended the same high school, which means we watched more high-school football games than we can count! Because both of our sons played on the team and both of our daughters made the cheerleading squad, our interest was more than casual. Those exciting autumn nights, the ecstasy of a last-minute winning touchdown pass, as well as the agony of a missed field goal—winning the championship as well as losing that final game—these are among our most cherished family memories.

During our years in the bleachers, we sat in the rooting section and screamed ourselves hoarse on more than a few occasions. Surrounded by other parents with an equally dedicated interest in the game, we often found ourselves completely caught up in the action on the field. My all-time favorite place to sit was near the father of our team's quarterback.

That father-son connection was truly something to behold. Now, understand that the boy on the field could not actually hear his dad in the stands. Nevertheless, the father kept up an amazing "running dialogue" as he encouraged his son to press on . . . to be tough . . . to get that ball down the field.

Sometimes it seemed uncanny how the dad (who had memorized all the plays) would call the next play and the son would do exactly as he was "told." I remember laughing as that intense dad would mumble words of positive affirmation. Seemingly in response, the boy would pick himself up after a sack and march the team right down the field to victory. I have even turned around and congratulated the volunteer coach in the stands for his incredible game plan!

In all our years of attending high-school football games, I

never heard the father of a player stand up and shout, "Take my son outta there! He's doing a terrible job! Put him on the bench!"

Of course not! Why? Because it is the most natural tendency of fathers to *exhort, encourage,* and *implore* their sons. Good dads affirm, they never condemn and attack their children. They believe in them to the very end.

And so it is with good leaders. With enthusiastic and reassuring words of affirmation, they help others to continue to believe in themselves, to do their very best.

Good dads affirm, they never condemn and attack their children.
They believe in them to the very end.

And so it is with good leaders.

Chapter 16

UNDER HIS LEADERSHIP

With care and concern for God's counsel on leadership, we have gone to the most reliable Book in the world to find guidelines worth following. We have discovered ways to inspire and influence others that result in a greater desire to cooperate and a deeper commitment to get the job done.

If you are serious about wanting to make a lasting and beneficial impact in others' lives as a leader uniquely used of God, I suggest that you regularly review the eight points I have just presented. Write them down on a card and put that card in a conspicuous place, perhaps on the visor of your car, under the glass at your desk, or on a mirror in your home. While going over the list, pray. Pray for the ability to carry out each of these objectives in the sphere of influence God has given you. Ask for patience, for wisdom, for determination, and for the ability to remain calm.

Then, as your day unfolds, maintain a three-dimensional perspective:

- *Look in.* Reflect on the value of being a person of strong inner security.
- *Look around.* Realize that a commitment to excellence requires tenacity of purpose.
- *Look up.* Remember that you are not alone . . . that the Lord of heaven is still in control.

This is a perfect opportunity to mention the importance of a strong faith. It is easy for determined leaders to omit the spiritual dimension while pursuing a successful career. Other involvements can seem so much more important that you'll be tempted to put this one off until later.

To conclude my comments on leadership, allow me to introduce to you another leader who knew all about the world so familiar to most leaders. His name is Howard Rutledge.

While an American Air Force pilot, Rutledge was shot down over North Vietnam during the early part of the Vietnam War. For several miserable years, Howard Rutledge endured unspeakable mistreatment at the hands of brutal captors. Following his release at the end of the war, he reflected upon those years when his life was reduced to torturous silence and intolerable loneliness.

During those longer periods of enforced reflection it became so much easier to separate the important from the trivial, the worthwhile from the waste. For example, in the past I usually worked or played hard on Sundays and had no time for church. For years Phyllis [his wife] had encouraged me to join the family at church. She never nagged or scolded—she just kept hoping. But I was too busy, too preoccupied, to spend one or two short hours a week thinking about the really important things.

Now the sights and sounds and smells of death were all around me. My hunger for spiritual food soon outdid my hunger for a steak. Now I wanted to know about that part of me that will never die. Now I wanted to talk about God and Christ and the church. But in Heartbreak [the name POWs gave their prison camp] solitary confinement, there was no pastor, no Sunday School teacher, no Bible, no hymnbook, no community of believers to guide and sustain me. I had completely neglected the spiritual dimension of my life. It took prison to show me how empty life is without God.[1]

You are not a prisoner of war as you read these words. Unless I miss my bet, you're not in solitary confinement either. Chances are good that your life is moving along at a pretty fast clip, perhaps so fast you've not taken the time to separate "the worthwhile from the waste," as Rutledge puts it. You may also have "completely neglected the spiritual dimension" of your life—a common yet tragic occurrence among busy leaders-in-the-making.

Turn your life over to the only One who can bring order and peace. His name is *Jesus*.

If so, pause and reflect. Then, like a good leader, be decisive. Turn your life over to the only One who can bring order and peace.

His name is Jesus.

To be a leader under His leadership, to serve as an officer in His army, to influence the lives around you under His influence, makes it all worthwhile. And no matter how great the trials, no matter how intense the pressure, no matter how many arrows fly, it will never, never have been in vain.

Part Three
Keep Your Balance:

~ •• ~

Remembering Compassion in a Careless World

*W*e have various ways to describe it. Turning the cheek. Going the extra mile. Doing good to those who hate us. Loving our enemies. Pouring coals of fire on another's head.

We may say it in different ways, but the action amounts to the same thing. By doing the *unexpected,* we accomplish a twofold objective: (1) we put an end to bitterness, and (2) we prove the truth of the age-old axiom *Love conquers all.*

I've seen it happen over and over again. I've also seen occasions when it could have worked, but neither side was willing to give it a whirl.

Why are we so hesitant? What keeps us from doing the unexpected for the undeserving so that we might watch God accomplish the unbelievable? What robs us of our peripheral vision, so that we jog on toward the mountain peaks shining on the horizon ahead of us but refuse to notice needy ones struggling through the thickets alongside the road?

Why do we wrestle with these things? Because compassion goes against our human nature. Furthermore, it's a major risk. Of course, that is where faith comes in: to believe the Lord against all odds and to obey Him even if the action backfires.

Someone reading this chapter may be frowning, thinking, *Yeah, that sounds good, but nobody could pull it off.* You are wrong, my friend. A few good men and women through the years have indeed pulled it off.

Joseph did.

After suffering years of abuse brought on by his hateful brothers' mistreatment, he lived to see the day when the tables were turned. Joseph was powerful, wealthy, respected, and surrounded by bodyguards. His brothers were weak, broke, unprotected, guilty to the core. It was his moment to unleash his rage and retribution. And these guys had it coming . . . in spades!

That is where faith comes in: to believe the Lord against all odds and to obey Him even if the action backfires.

Instead, the son of Jacob and Rachel did the unexpected. His action shocked his brothers down to their worn-out sandals. After all those years of guilt and dread and self-recrimination, he wasn't going to spring a get-even attack? Not even a tongue-lashing? As it turned out, those who so richly deserved hatred and retribution received love and forgiveness. And the rest is history . . . beautiful, beautiful history.

Even as I write these words, I can sense some cynic's shrug: *Well, that was then, this is now. No one would ever do that today.* How wrong you are.

Rabbi Michael Weisser did. It happened in Lincoln, Nebraska, where for more than three years, Larry Trapp, a self-proclaimed Nazi and Ku Klux Klansman, spread vicious hatred through mailings and phone calls. He promoted white supremacy, anti-Semitism, and other messages of prejudice, declaring his apartment the KKK state headquarters and himself the grand dragon.

Weisser became one of Trapp's targets, receiving dozens of pieces of hate mail and offensive phone calls. At first, the Weissers were so afraid they locked their doors and worried themselves sick over the safety of their family. Trapp, a forty-two-year-old, clinically blind, double-amputee, continued to spew out his racial slurs and obscene remarks.

Then one day Rabbi Weisser decided to do the unexpected.

He left a message on Trapp's answering machine, telling the man of another side of life . . . a life free of hatred and racism. "I probably called ten times and left messages before he finally picked up the phone and asked me why I was harassing him. I said I'd like to help him. I offered him a ride to the grocery store."

Trapp was stunned. Disarmed by the unexpected kindness and courtesy, he started thinking. He later admitted, through tears, that he heard in the rabbi's voice "something I hadn't experienced. It was love."

Slowly the bitter man began to soften. One night he called the Weissers and said he wanted out . . . but didn't know how. They grabbed a bucket of fried chicken and took him dinner. Before long they made a trade: In return for their love he gave them his swastika rings, hate tracts, and Klan robes. That same day Trapp gave up his recruiting job and dumped the rest of his propaganda in the trash.

"They showed me so much love that I couldn't help but love them back," he finally confessed.

Still unconvinced?

Consider what happened to Pastor Philip (Flip) Benham, head of the prolife organization Operation Rescue, in Dallas, Texas. He's another man who could tell you about the unexpected results of compassion. The story really began a few years ago after the national headquarters of Operation Rescue moved in next door to (of all places) a Dallas women's health clinic.

They showed me so much love that I couldn't help but love them back.

It was there that Benham first encountered Norma McCorvey, who worked at the clinic—the same Norma McCorvey named as the "Jane Roe" of the Supreme Court's tragic *Roe v. Wade* decision in 1973, legalizing abortion.

Now you might imagine that two such individuals in such close proximity might generate a significant amount of hostility. After all, this was the same woman who (in a reporter's hearing) invited a critic who accused her of killing babies to "Bring yours over here and we'll do them too."

At first, the relationship was as tense as you might expect. Recriminations bounced back and forth across the protest lines. Knowing how passionately Benham felt about this issue, you could certainly imagine him shouting at this "poster child of the proabortion movement"—or pointing at her and accusing her of gross crimes against humanity.

But Benham didn't do that. Instead, he lowered his defenses, cooled the rhetoric, and simply began talking to the woman. He took an interest in her. He listened to her. He showed compassion. The two became unlikely friends, and Norma began to slowly reveal the secret doubts that plagued her heart.

The sight of empty swings in a playground one afternoon suddenly gripped her. She later told ABC News, "They were swinging back and forth, but they were all empty, and I just totally lost it. And I thought, *Oh my God, the playgrounds are empty because there's no children, because they've all been aborted.*"

Within a few weeks, Norma McCorvey began visiting the offices of her "adversaries," even volunteering to do a few odd jobs. It didn't make any earthly sense, but the folks at Operation Rescue showed her courtesy, warmth, and friendship. When seven-year-old Emily, daughter of the office manager, invited the woman she now calls "Auntie" to church, McCorvey accepted. And that very night she found Jesus Christ as her Savior.

Now Norma volunteers at Operation Rescue and has become an outspoken opponent of the cause she once defended so fiercely. As a correspondent from the *Washington Times* reported, "[Norma] prays, sometimes from 1 A.M. to 3 A.M. 'How is it I can serve You?' she asks God. 'How can I please You and make You smile on me?'"

It all began with a man who had every logical reason for showing a woman hate, scorn, and rejection. But showed her love instead.

In the pages of Scripture, the Lord Jesus told a story about just such an event. And as we consider it together, we'll learn what it means to keep our balance in this weary, wounded world we call home. We'll learn that we can reach for the heights of leadership and victory . . . without forgetting those broken men and women alongside the road.

Chapter 17

THE LORD SETS THE STAGE

et's flash back to the first century, where the Man called Jesus met with real men and women in the streets and marketplaces of Palestine.

On one particular street, among the crowds of onlookers, stood a lawyer. Like all lawyers, he was trained to think, to examine the evidence, to probe for the flaw, to ask the hard questions. After observing the scene sufficiently, the attorney decided to ask a pointed question. "Teacher, what shall I do to inherit eternal life?" (Luke 10:25).

What a question! In thirty-eight years of ministry, I could count on both hands (and would have fingers left over) the times I've been directly asked that question. I'm telling you, I would love to answer that question.

But the beautiful thing about our Lord's answer is that it was so profound, so *unexpected* (there's that word again). It wasn't at all the predictable, pat answer you might expect today. As a matter of fact, His answer came in the form of another question. "What is written in the Law? How does it read to you?" (Luke 10:26).

Perhaps Jesus had noticed something the man was wearing. In those days the strict scribes (first-century lawyers) wore little leather pouches on their wrists into which they placed selected statements from the Torah. These pouches were called "phylacteries." Jesus may have seen this lawyer's phylacteries and realized that within them was the very answer for which the man was searching.

The lawyer answered the Lord's probing question swiftly and succinctly: "You shall love the Lord your God with all your heart, and with all your soul, and with all your strength, and with all your mind; and your neighbor as yourself" (Luke 10:27).

Drawing his answer from two sections of the Law, the attorney wasted no time in delivering a dead-on-target response.

No one from the crowd interrupted the interchange. I imagine it seemed as if the scribe and the Savior stood alone on the street, their eyes locked on each other . . . both concentrating on the subject, neither allowing his mind to wander. Onlookers must have wondered how the Nazarene would respond to such a quick and concise answer. And they probably breathed a sigh of relief when they heard—"You have answered correctly" (10:28).

⌒ ∞ ⌐

How do you define "neighbor?"

But I'm certain the next statement turned all eyes back toward the scribe, almost as if the crowd were following a verbal tennis match.

"Do this and you will live."

Suddenly the ball bounced back to the lawyer's court. And if I know anything about lawyers, they don't like to see the ball returned! They much prefer serving to returning. I can't help but wonder if the man didn't squirm. No doubt he liked hearing the "You have answered correctly" part.

It was the "Do this" comment that forced his hand.

Notice that Dr. Luke adds an insightful tidbit before recording the lawyer's next volley: "But wishing to justify himself, he said to Jesus, 'And who is my neighbor?' " (10:29).

This time the lawyer's question springs from a defensive spirit. The man felt the screws tightening, under the gun to produce. In effect, Jesus had said, "You want eternal life? You're interested in the life I'm offering that will be distinctly different? Then you should know up front that it will have a *drastic* effect on you, both vertically (with God), and horizontally (with your neighbor)."

The vertical part, of course, could be faked. (Who could ever produce evidence that he failed at loving the Lord his God with all his heart and mind and strength?) But the horizontal? When it came to loving his neighbor—ah, there was the rub!

So, good attorney that he was, he retreated to lawyerly language and began picking at the terms. He said, in effect, "How do you DEFINE 'neighbor' "?

He'd understood Jesus' sentence, all right. But didn't that term *neighbor* give him a lot of wobble room?

"Who, pray tell, is one's neighbor? Is it just the fella next door? Or two doors away? Or down around the corner? What if his skin is a different color from my own? What if she speaks a different language from mine? Does she qualify as my neighbor? You see, Teacher, that's a pretty vague term."

The dialogue in Luke 10 reminds me of a true story I heard theologian Carl F. H. Henry tell as he spoke to a group of radio broadcasters. The late Dr. Reinhold Niebuhr (no pun intended) decided to write out his theological position, stating exactly where he stood philosophically—his credo.

Being the profound thinker he was (and a bit verbose), it took him many sheets of paper to express himself. Upon completion of his masterwork, he realized it needed to be read and evaluated by a mind much more practical than his own. So he bundled up the material and sent it to a minister whom he knew possessed a practical mind and a pastoral "heart."

With great pains the clergyman sweated through this ream of paper, trying desperately to grasp the meaning. When he finally finished, he worked up the nerve to write a brief yet absolutely candid note in reply. It read:

> My dear Dr. Niebuhr:
> I understand every word you have written, but I do not understand *one* sentence.[1]

I suggest that the opposite problem plagued the first-century attorney. He understood the sentence but floundered at the word *neighbor.* So he asked a question he thought might put the matter to rest.

But it didn't.

Chapter 18

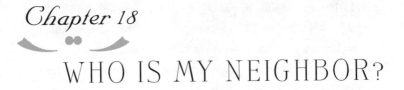

WHO IS MY NEIGHBOR?

*J*f I live to be one hundred and fifty years old, I will still be impressed with the way Jesus answered the lawyer's question. Rather than digging into the etymology of the term or rebuking the guy for defensiveness, He simply told a story. As with all of Jesus' stories, this one appeared harmless, almost childlike. But behind it lay a vast network of implications.

The little story immediately caught the lawyer's attention because of its familiar setting. Read it, please, as if for the first time:

Jesus replied and said, "A certain man was going down from Jerusalem to Jericho; and he fell among robbers, and they stripped him and beat him, and went off leaving him half dead. And by chance a certain priest was going down on that road, and when he saw him, he passed by on the other side. And like-wise a Levite also, when he came to the place and saw him, passed by on the other side. But a certain Samaritan, who was on a journey, came upon him; and when he saw him, he felt compassion, and came to him, and bandaged up his wounds, pouring oil and wine on them; and he put him on his own beast, and brought him to an inn, and took care of him. And on the next day he took out two denarii and gave them to the innkeeper and said, 'Take care of him; and whatever more you spend, when I return, I will repay you.'" (Luke 10:30–35)

THE SETTING

Between Jerusalem and Jericho stretched twenty miles of bad road. Not only did it drop twenty-three hundred feet in ele-vation, but it harbored a notorious "alley" where thieves, rapists, and other criminal types hung out. The twists and turns in the rugged road provided them places to surprise their vic-tims and carry out their vicious crimes.

I don't know of a metropolis in America without a few places that are unsafe to travel alone. Some urban areas boast just a few mean streets; others, like New York City, Chicago, Houston, and Los Angeles, contain sprawling sections from which the general public stays away. In such neighborhoods, the only safe time to go for a walk is when the police hold their annual parade—and you are marching in it!

The Jericho highway was like that. Every Jew for miles around knew it. So when Jesus started His story by describing a man who traveled that road, every listener no doubt antici-pated that trouble lay ahead.

The Victim

Predictably, the man in the story was assaulted, stripped, beaten, and left like so much carrion alongside the road. According to Jesus, the robbers "went off leaving him half dead."

Now, it's important to remember that this story grows out of the lawyer's question, "Who is my neighbor?" Interestingly, we are never told the origin of the victim. We assume he was a Jew, perhaps a Jerusalem resident, but we have no idea where he lived. He is called merely "a certain man"—nothing more.

Two Fellow Travelers

Three others who also traveled the Jericho highway that day *are* identified. Each saw the victim in his desperate situation, although none knew him. Let's consider the first two.

The first was "a certain priest." This man traveled the road and saw the man, but when he saw him, he deliberately walked away from him. He "passed by on the other side."

That's not hard to understand, is it? Ministers are busy people with schedules to keep, deadlines to meet, sermons to prepare. And who could blame the priest for fearing that he might fall into a trap? Furthermore, if we were to get technical about it, we could remind ourselves that the priest had an excuse. He was not to be "ceremonially contaminated" by touching someone in such a rough state. After all, he needed to keep his equilibrium and not get "carried away" by every person in need.

Next, a Levite came along. Perhaps we'd be in the ballpark if we thought of him as an assistant minister discipled by the priest. He, too, invested his life in his work. He had people to meet, programs to plan, functions to arrange, ceremonial requirements to fulfill. So we really shouldn't be surprised that he also "passed by on the other side" when he caught a glance of the bleeding victim. He may have even thought, *Poor guy . . . if only I had time to stop.*

But there was no time, it seems. So the Levite hurried on.

Before moving to the third traveler, let me mention an event that actually occurred on the campus of an evangelical seminary, the very grounds where future ministers received their training. A professor assigned his Greek class to study Luke 10:25–37—the Good Samaritan story we are considering. These young theologs were to analyze the biblical text in depth, observing and commenting on all the major terms and syntactical factors worth mentioning. Each student was then to write his own translation of the story.

As is true in most language classes, a few of the students cared more about the practical implications of the assignment than its intellectual aspects. On the morning their work was to be turned in, three students teamed up to carry out a memorable object lesson. One volunteered to play the part of a victim. The other two tore his shirt and trousers, rubbed mud, catsup, and other realistic-looking ingredients across his "wounds," marked up his eyes and face so he hardly resembled himself, then placed him along the path that led from the dormitory to the Greek classroom.

While his friends hid and watched, he groaned and writhed, simulating great pain.

Not one student stopped.

The seminarians walked around him, stepped over him,

and made various statements to him. But nobody stooped over to help. What do you want to bet their academic work was flawless, insightful, and handed in on time?

This incident always reminds me of a scripture that presses us relentlessly beyond our merely intellectual concerns: "We know love by this, that He laid down His life for us; and we ought to lay down our lives for the brethren. But whoever has the world's goods, and beholds his brother in need and closes his heart against him, how does the love of God abide in him?" (1 John 3:16–17).

It also reminds me of a scene out of *Winnie the Pooh*. Pooh Bear is walking along the riverbank. Eeyore, his stuffed donkey friend, suddenly appears floating downstream . . . on his back of all things, obviously troubled about the possibility of drowning.

Pooh calmly asks if Eeyore had fallen in. Trying to appear in complete control, the anguished donkey answers, "Silly of me, wasn't it." Pooh disregards his friend's pleading eyes and remarks that Eeyore really should have been more careful.

In greater need than ever, Eeyore politely thanks him for the advice (even though he needs action more than words). Almost with a yawn, Pooh Bear notices, "I think you are sinking." With that as his only hint of hope, drowning Eeyore asks Pooh if he would mind rescuing him. So, Pooh pulls him from the river. Eeyore apologizes for being such a bother, and Pooh, still unconcerned, yet ever so courteous, responds, "Don't be silly . . . you should have said something sooner."[1]

I find it amazing how closely that episode reflects our world of real people in real need. How many Eeyores there are, soaked to the ears and about to drown—yet we keep ourselves safely separated with nice-sounding questions and courteous remarks! We'll even say, "Give me a call if you need me."

Yeah, right.

Honestly now, when's the last time someone in need actually "gave you a call"? Do you really believe that will ever happen? And even if someone did work up the courage to pick up the phone, would you be serious about helping? We learn early how to say all the right words, yet deep down mean *none* of them.

ONE COMPASSIONATE SAMARITAN

The average citizen may not care much about the other fellow, but a few marvelous exceptions do exist, like this third man Jesus mentioned. It is important to realize that his race and heritage play a significant part in Jesus' story.

Bluntly, he was a half-breed. True Jews so hated the Samaritans that they refused all contact with them. They hated the thought of even having Samaritan dust soil their sandals. If a Judean down South planned to visit Galilee up North, since Samaria lay smack dab in the middle of that journey, he went *around* it, rather than through it.

To help picture the deep hatreds of this ancient hostility, I once drew an analogy from our own United States. I said this would be like a Texan traveling to Kansas, but detouring around Oklahoma. After the meeting three massive men, each well over 250 pounds and not one shorter than six feet, four inches, cornered me. They identified themselves as Oklahoma Sooners and informed me (jokingly), "We jus' wanna make it clear that we ain't got no Samaritans in Oklahoma!"

I smiled as I drove home that night, realizing that not even today are Samaritans free of prejudice. Then my thoughts grew more serious as I reflected on our Lord's story.

You can be sure that when the lawyer heard Jesus mention "a certain Samaritan" on the Jericho road, the hair on the back of his neck stood up.

Remember that Jesus told this story to answer the lawyer's question, "Who is my neighbor?" But as the story progressed, it became obvious to everyone that His answer must not be connected to geography . . . or race . . . or lifestyle. Difficult and distasteful as it must have been for the attorney to accept, he was forced to hear that the Jewish victim was assisted by none other than a Samaritan stranger.

All three of the men in Jesus' story "saw" the one who had been stripped, beaten, and abandoned. But only one, the half-breed Samaritan, *felt compassion* for the man.

Compassion is what set the Samaritan apart from the other two. Compassion was the connecting link, the magnet, that drew him to the helpless victim.

Even today, that's what compassion does.

Invariably, compassion says, "Get involved. Reach out. Risk. You can't ignore this person's needs. You care too much

❧ •• ❧

> Compassion is what set the Samaritan apart from the other two.

to walk away." Another New Testament writer sees compassion as that which makes Christianity authentic. Like a one-sided coin, faith without works is counterfeit.

Listen to how James says it: "Now what use is it, my brothers, for a man to say he 'has faith' if his actions do not correspond with it? Could that sort of faith save anyone's soul? If a fellow man or woman has no clothes to wear and nothing to eat, and one of you says, 'Good luck to you, I hope you'll keep warm and find enough to eat,' and yet gives them nothing to meet their physical needs, what on earth is the good of that?" (James 2:14–16, PHILLIPS).

Obviously, the Samaritan in Jesus' story demonstrated authentic faith. His compassion went to work. Consider his genuine concern.

- He came to the victim.
- He bandaged up the stranger's wounds.
- He poured oil and wine on the injuries.
- He put the stranger on his own beast.
- He stayed the night, taking care of the man.
- He picked up the tab, even promising to return and pay whatever other expenses might be incurred (something like leaving your Visa card with the innkeeper).

As far as we know, the Samaritan never spoke a word of compassion to the wounded traveler. He just rolled up his sleeves and *demonstrated* it.

Chapter 19

A KEY QUESTION

s Jesus concluded His story, He no doubt peered intently into the lawyer's eyes as He asked the crucial question: "Which of these three do you think proved to be a neighbor to the man who fell into the robbers' hands?"

Wait a minute! That's a different question from the one that led to the story of the Good Samaritan. The original question was, "Who is my neighbor?" By requesting a definition—cold, objective, distant, hypothetical—the lawyer thought he would be safe as he searched the horizon for that special (and rare) individual who qualified as "my neighbor."

But Jesus refused to fan an irrelevant flame. The Master shifted the emphasis so that the only question worth considering at the end of the story was not "Which person qualifies as *my* neighbor?" but "What kind of neighbor *am I?*"

You see, that question points the finger in the other direction—in the lawyer's direction, in your direction, in my direction.

To put it another way, the appropriate question is not "Is my neighbor really lost and therefore needy?" but rather, "Is my neighbor's neighbor—namely, me—really saved and therefore compassionate?"

Thankfully, the lawyer got the point. Which man proved to be a neighbor? "The one who showed mercy toward him." (Even then, however, the lawyer couldn't bring himself to say, "The Samaritan." All he could manage was, "The one who showed mercy." Some lessons seem almost impossible to learn!) And now Jesus is ready to deliver His point, an answer that has come full circle. Before the story He had told the scribe, "Do this and you will live" (Luke 10:28). Now He says virtually the same thing, "Go and do the same" (v. 37).

Our greatest need is not to hold back until we locate some special individual who qualifies as the one. Rather, it is to realize that needs exist all around us, each one awaiting a tangible demonstration of compassion. Our involvement proves we possess eternal life.

The only question worth considering at the end of the story was not "Which person qualifies as *my* neighbor?" but *What kind of neighbor am I?*

I doubt there is anything more basic, more Christlike, and therefore more Christian than compassion. Yet many of us who call ourselves "evangelical" miss this truth. In place of compassion we have deliberately substituted information. Somehow we have concluded that knowledge heals wounds. We have convinced ourselves that what the hurting soul really needs are facts.

When did we buy into such heresy?

Where, pray tell, do we find Christ modeling any such thing? Don't misunderstand—biblical truth *is* important, doctrinal knowledge *is* valuable. But those truths come later, *after* mercy has won a hearing ... *after* compassion has prepared the soil into which truth can take root.

This fact struck me in a fresh way at a pastors' conference a number of years ago.

It began with one of those backhanded compliments, the kind that makes you pause, think, then respond, rather than gush out a quick, "Hey, thanks." The guy had listened to me during several of the sessions. We had not met before, so all he knew about me was what he'd heard in the past few days: ex-Marine ... Texan ... schooled in an independent seminary ... committed to biblical exposition ... premil ... pretrib ... pro this ... anti that. You know how all those scary labels go.

I think he expected your basic, squeaky-clean preacher: dark suit; white shirt and tie; scuffed wing-tips; a big study Bible with lots of tiny-print footnotes; a deep frown; thunderous shouts; and a rather large fist flailing away in midair.

Since that's not what he got, he felt as if I threw him a low curve over the inside corner of the pulpit. Finally, toward the end of the week, he decided to drink a cup of coffee with me and risk saying it straight. It went something like this:

"You don't fit. What's with you? You've got the roots of a fundamentalist, but you don't sound like it. Your theology is narrow, but you're not rigid. You take God seriously but laugh like there's no tomorrow. You have definite convictions, but you aren't legalistic and demanding."

Then he added: "Even though you're a firm believer in the Bible, you're still having fun, still enjoying life. You've even got some *compassion.*"

That did it. By then both of us were laughing out loud. A few eyes from other tables flashed us those "Would you two quiet down!" looks. I often encounter such glares. Especially when I'm having fun.

Well, what could I say? The man could have been a lot more severe, but he had me pretty well pegged. It was that last statement, however, that really got me thinking. It woke me up the next morning.

"You've even got compassion."

As though it was not supposed to be there! As if a commitment to the truth of Scripture somehow rules out a deep concern for people. You know, that messy human stuff—

Even though you're a firm believer in the Bible, you're still having fun, still enjoying life. You've even got some *compassion.*

heartaches, hunger, illness, fractured lives, struggles with insecurities, failures, and grief—because those are only "temporal problems." Mere horizontal hassles. Leave that to the liberals. Our main job is to give 'em the gospel! Get 'em saved. Don't get sidetracked by their pain and problems. It's *conversion* we're really interested in, not compassion. Once they're born again and get into the Word, all those other things will solve themselves.

Right? Be honest now. Isn't that the way it is many times? Isn't it a fact that the more conservative one becomes, the less compassionate? I know there are some exceptions, but we're talking about the general rule.

I want to know why. Why either-or? Why not both-and?

I'd also like to know *when*.

When did we depart from the biblical model?

When did we begin to ignore Christ's care for the needy?

When did we stop thinking of how valuable it is to be healing agents and wound wrappers, as with the Good Samaritan?

When did we opt for placing more emphasis on being proclaimers and defenders and less on becoming repairers and restorers?

When did we decide to strengthen our focus on public announcements and weaken our involvement in private assistance?

Maybe when we realized that one is much easier than the other. It's also faster. And neater. And less complicated. When you don't concern yourself with being your brother's keeper, you don't have to get dirty or take risks or lose your objectivity or run up against the thorny side of an issue that lacks easy answers.

And what will happen when we choose to follow Christ and traffic in such compassion? *The Living Bible* says: "Then the Lord will be your delight, and I will see to it that you ride high, and get your full share of the blessings I promised to Jacob, your father. The Lord has spoken" (Isaiah 58:14).

Yes, He has spoken. But have we heard?

If I could put this whole chapter into one sentence, it would be:

OTHERS WILL NOT CARE
HOW MUCH WE KNOW
UNTIL THEY KNOW HOW MUCH WE CARE.

Please say that out loud. Pull it forward until it rests, simmering, on the front burner of your mind. It is true! But putting it to the test in our lives will require an active reaching out beyond our safe and protective wall. And reach out we must. As one authority puts it:

We are fully ourselves only in relation to the other; the I detached from a Thou disintegrates. I do not find you by chance; I find you by an active life of reaching out.[1]

Chapter 20

~ •• ~

INSIGHTFUL PERCEPTION

*P*eople with compassion reach out because they perceive needs. And most needs are not nearly so obvious as the Jericho road victim. The people we bump up against may be equally "stripped, beaten, and abandoned," but most of their needs they keep locked up inside—behind walls of pseudo-security, hidden beneath masks that smile and say, "Fine, I'm just fine." But more often than not, lurking behind those masks are massive fears and fragile feelings of insecurity.

Compassionate Samaritan types aren't fooled by such smoke screens. They refuse to walk away, mouthing the glib yet popular farewell, "Have a nice day." One author has spoken honestly and vulnerably with these penetrating admissions:

> Don't be fooled by me. Don't be fooled by the face I wear. I wear a mask. I wear a thousand masks—masks that I am afraid to take off; and none of them are me.

Pretending is an art that is second nature to me, but don't be fooled. For my sake, don't be fooled. I give the impression that I am secure, that all is sunny and unruffled within me as well as without; that confidence is my name and coolness is my game, that the water is calm and I am in command; and that I need no one. But don't believe me, please. My surface may seem smooth, but my surface is my mask, my ever-varying and ever-concealing mask.

Beneath lies no smugness, no complacence. Beneath dwells the real me in confusion, in fear, in aloneness. But I hide that. I don't want anybody to know it. I panic at the thought of my weakness and fear being exposed. That's why I frantically create a mask to hide behind—a nonchalant, sophisticated façade—to help me pretend, to shield me from the glance that he knows. But such a glance is precisely my salvation, my only salvation and I know it. That is, if it's followed by acceptance. If it's followed by love.

It's the only thing that liberates me from myself, from my own self-built prison wall, from the barriers I so painstakingly erect. It's the only thing that will assure me of what I can't assure myself—that I am really something. . . .

~ •• ~

That's why I frantically create a mask to hide behind—a nonchalant, sophisticated façade—to help me pretend.

Who am I, you may wonder. I am someone you know very well. I am every man you meet. I am every woman you meet. I am every child you meet. I am right in front of you. Please . . . love me.[1]

Compassionate people understand and accept those words. They possess "the glance that knows" as well as the love and acceptance that mask-wearing strugglers need in order to feel secure enough to drop their guard. They are truly remarkable and rare individuals.

As a result, they become welcoming harbors for discouraged men, women, and kids seeking shelter from the storm. A place of safety. A refuge.

Chapter 21

BECOMING
A PERSON OF REFUGE

*I*f I were to mention the word "refugee," you would most likely picture some hazy, distant land—perhaps Rwanda or Serbia—where crowds of frightened, disheveled men, women, and children crowd the dirt roads, possessions strapped to their backs.

Far too often in this broken world, that truly is an accurate picture. But in this context, when I mention refugees, I don't necessarily have in mind those who cross borders—or even oceans—to find protection from "ethnic cleansing" or a government gone mad.

I'm thinking about someone nearby rather than far away. Someone you see in the course of your day, rather than an image on a flat television screen or staring up at you from the pages of a magazine.

I simply mean someone who needs a refuge. A place of

shelter. I'm talking about a person who is broken or guilty or bleeding with a heartache or exploding with anxiety. Or all of the above.

Back in the days when the Hebrews settled Canaan, they set up cities of refuge. People who were in danger—even those guilty of wrongdoing—could escape to one of these seven cities and find personal relief and refreshment.

Don't misunderstand. These weren't sleazy dumping grounds for hardened criminals. They were territories dedicated to the restoration of those who had made mistakes. People who had blown it could flee to one of these places of refuge and expect that no one inside would throw rocks at them. Rather, they could admit their faults and not be threatened by pious looks or caustic sermons from prejudiced lips.

Which reminds me of an old marine buddy of mine who came to know Christ after he was discharged from the Corps. I was pleasantly surprised when I heard about this because he wasn't your basic, clean-cut, Little Lord Fauntleroy type. Back when we were in the same outfit, he cursed loudly, drank heavily, fought hard, chased women, loved weapons and war, and hated chapel services. In short, he made a great marine.

Back then he and God weren't on speaking terms. But then—miracle of miracles—through a chain of events too lengthy to describe, the guy was converted. Christ came into his life.

I'll never forget the day we ran into each other. He put his hand on my shoulder, sighed, and said, "Chuck, I'll be honest. The only thing I really miss is that old fellowship all the guys in our outfit used to have down at the slop shoot [Greek for "tavern on the base"]. All the guys would sit around, laugh, tell stories, drink a pitcher of beer, and really let our hair down. Man, it was great! I just haven't found anything to take the place of those times . . . and I still need it! I ain't got nobody to tell my troubles to, to admit my faults to . . . to have 'em listen when I need to say, 'I'm sunk. I'm beat. I've had it.' There isn't anybody who will put his arm around me and tell me I'm still okay. Somebody who will keep my secrets and help me get back up.'"

That man is a refugee in need of a refuge—but sadly, refuges in the Christian community are hard to find. The supply and demand has broken down. Like modern-day priests and Levites, we pass by people like this (with a nod and a smile) on the left and right.

We believers have lots of places to meet and sing. To hear talks from big wooden pulpits. To watch fine people sing and pray and read from the Book.

But where do the escapes go?

Where do the wounded turn?

We have a place for the healthy and productive. We love to use the gifted, the leader types, the strong, and the confident. But where is our compassion? Where is the place of refuge for

Like modern-day priests and Levites, we pass by people like this (with a nod and a smile) on the left and right.

those who have gotten soiled in the streets? Rather than being committed to restoration, we bypass the dirty with a shrug. Sometimes even thinking, *I'm not surprised.*

More often than we want to admit, we're bad Samaritans.

In our outfit we're notorious for not knowing what to do with our wounded. Getting in there and cleaning up those ugly wounds and changing bloody bandages and taking the time to listen and encourage, well . . . let's be practical, we're not running a hospital around here.

That makes good sense until you or I need emergency care.

Like when you discover your husband is a practicing homosexual. Or your unmarried daughter is pregnant and isn't listening to you. Or your parent is an alcoholic. Or you get dumped in jail for shoplifting. Or you drive your finances into a ditch. Or you lose your job—and it's your own fault. Or your wife is having an affair. Or your dad or mom or mate or child is dying of cancer.

Thankfully, there are a few lights in the church to help the hurting find their way back. In my opinion they are the brightest hope on our horizon.

Thankfully, there are a few lights in the church to help the hurting find their way back. In my opinion, they are the brightest hope on our horizon.

I think about some of the open caring and honest sharing in the Promise Keeper conferences. Or the group that meets weekly to help people who struggle to conquer alcohol and drug addiction . . . brave souls who admit by their presence, "We don't have it all together." Or the group of single parents who are attempting to believe in themselves again as much as they believe in Jesus. Besides these, small groups in churches across our land are dedicated to growing friendships and deepening relationships. Good Samaritans who practice compassion.

Listen, when the bottom drops out, people don't want to listen to a cassette of some sermon. Books are fine, but nothing takes the place of personal presence. Your presence. Wounded people need a place to cry . . . a person to care . . . someone to bind up their wounds . . . someone to listen . . . the security of a few close, intimate friends who won't blab their story all over the church . . . who will do more than say, "I'll pray for you."

What they want is a *refuge*. What they need is a believer who thinks more about their needs than his or her own comfort and convenience.

Even as I write these words, I'm reminded of someone who modeled Christlike compassion for me more than anyone I've ever met. I'm thinking of my own older brother, Orville.

Chapter 22

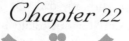

A PERSONAL ILLUSTRATION

*O*rville Swindoll is a veteran missionary in Buenos Aires
. . . a man of great intellect and an even greater heart
for God. Among my earliest memories from our
home, I distinctly recall awakening in the middle of the night
and seeing Orville on his knees in prayer.

You may not like to read this, but I resented his "fanatical"
relationship with God. I remember thinking, *What a drag. Why
couldn't I have a "normal" brother who plays football, letters in several
sports, and likes to fish and hunt? How come I'm stuck with this
teenage monk instead of a red-blooded all-American?*

I have long since come to realize just how valuable
Orville's life really was. And is. But back then I wrestled
deeply with such questions. To me, he was just too much.

It may help to set the scene if you understand that Orville,
my sister Luci, and I were reared by an extremely pragmatic

father. Say what you like about the walk of faith, my dad was too functional and practical to get very excited about totally trusting God. Don't get me wrong, he was a Christian. But he didn't buy into any extreme view of Christianity. To this day, I can hear him say, "It's okay to talk about faith and depending on the Lord, but God also gave you a brain, so use it. He gave you arms and muscles, so be responsible."

I suppose the statement, "There ain't no free spiritual lunch," says it best. My dad believed in hard work and taking care of what you owned and protecting yourself from nuts and ripoff artists. "Don't be foolish. Fight laziness. If you've got shoes, keep 'em shined. If you own a car, keep it clean. Don't slam the door. Make your bed. Mow the grass. Don't pick up hitchhikers. Choose your friends carefully. Never mess around with guys who drink, fast girls, total strangers (especially ex-cons), people who borrow money, or loud-mouthed, fast-talking salesmen."

You get the picture. But Orville had trouble when those "rules" bumped up against the walk of faith. Allow me to jump ahead a few years.

When my brother was mustered out of the navy, he drove from the Great Lakes area toward Houston. While en route, he picked up a stranger, somewhere on a bleak, windy Kansas highway. The hitchhiker, after hours of trudging through the cold, was delighted to take a seat in a warm car. It wasn't long before the two of them got on the subject of spiritual things.

The man had led a rugged life and had recently been released from prison. The black backdrop of his past provided Orville with a perfect canvas upon which to paint the beautiful message of Christ's death for sinners and His offer of forgiveness and eternal life to all who believe.

My brother's winsome, personal approach, mixed with his authentic compassion for the man in need, proved irresistible. The man quietly and humbly took the gift and became a "new creature in Christ."

By the time the two of them reached central Oklahoma, the stranger announced he was near his home; he would get off here. As he opened the door, a wintry blast filled the car.

"Where's your coat?" asked Orville.

"Well, I don't have one . . . but I'll be fine."

"Wait a minute," Orville said. With that, my brother reached into his seabag and dug out his Navy pea jacket. You remember that dark blue, double-breasted, big-collar government issue every sailor wore on cold days? He tossed the jacket toward the stranger with a smile.

"Here's your new coat."

Shivering, the man buttoned it up, then leaned through the door and, with real feeling, said, "In all my life I've never met anyone like you. How can I ever thank you enough?"

Meanwhile, back in Houston, my dad awaited the arrival of his older son. Clipboard in hand. Ready to check off the seabag supplies. I was only a teenager at the time, but the scene has been indelibly printed in my museum of memories.

"Eight pairs of socks?"

"Check. Eight pairs."

"Three caps?"

"Check. Three caps."

"Six white T-shirts?"

"Check. Six T-shirts."

"Eight pairs of skivvies?"

"Check. Eight pairs."

"Two pairs of shoes?"

"Check. Two pairs."

"One pea jacket?"

"Uh . . . well. . . ."

My dad lowered the clipboard and looked into my brother's eyes. "Where's the jacket?"

"It's not here, Dad."

"I can see that! Where is it?"

"Well, it's somewhere in central Oklahoma."

"Oklahoma? Did you lose it?"

"No, actually I gave it away."

"To whom?"

Swallowing hard, Orville took a deep breath, and then spoke with calm confidence. "Dad, I gave it to a hitchhiker I picked up in Kansas. He had just gotten out of prison and he didn't have a coat. So I gave him mine."

One incredible space of silence transpired as two strong-minded Swindolls locked eyes. Finally, my father leaned across the kitchen table, cleared his throat, and responded, "You know, Orville, I haven't understood you for a long time."

My brother—standing about three inches from Dad's nose—replied, "No, Dad. And I don't think you ever will."

Orville had trouble when those "rules" bumped up against the walk of faith.

I learned a never-to-be-forgotten lesson that afternoon. Truly compassionate people are often hard to understand. They take risks most people would never take. They give away what most people would cling to. They reach out and touch when most would hold back with folded arms. They don't usually operate on the basis of human logic, nor do they care overly much about rules of safety. Their caring brings them up close where they feel the other person's pain and do whatever is necessary to demonstrate true concern. An arm's length "be warmed and be filled" comment won't cut it.

As one understanding soul expressed it: "Compassion is not a snob gone slumming. Anyone can salve his conscience by an occasional foray into knitting for the spastic home. Did you ever take a real trip down inside the broken heart of a friend? To feel the sob of the soul—the raw, red crucible of emotional agony? To have this become almost as much yours as that of your soul-crushed neighbor? Then, to sit down with him—and silently weep? This is the beginning of compassion."[1]

Parceling out this kind of compassion will elicit no whistles or loud applause. Crawling into that "raw, red crucible" is no pastime for glory hogs. In fact, the best acts of compassion will never be known by the masses. Nor will fat sums of money be dumped into your lap because you are committed to being helpful. Only once in a blue moon will a Mother Teresa be awarded the Nobel Peace Prize. Normally, acts of mercy are done in obscurity with no thought (or receipt) of monetary gain.

A war correspondent paused long enough to watch a nun as she unwrapped a wounded soldier's leg. Gangrene had set in. The stench from the pus and blood so repulsed him that he turned away and mumbled under his breath, "I wouldn't do that for a million bucks."

The nun glanced up and replied, "Neither would I."

Would you? Is that what it would take? Ruth Harms Calkin touches a sensitive spot in all of us as she wonders—

> You know, Lord, how I serve You
> With great emotional fervor
> In the limelight.
> You know how eagerly I speak for You
> At a women's club.
> You know how I effervesce when I promote
> A fellowship group.
> You know my genuine enthusiasm
> At a Bible study.
> But how would I react, I wonder
> If you pointed to a basin of water
> And asked me to wash the calloused feet
> Of a bent and wrinkled old woman
> Day after day,
> Month after month,
> In a room where nobody saw
> And nobody knew?[2]

Compassion usually calls for a willingness to humbly spend oneself in obscurity on behalf of unknowns. How few there are in our fast-paced, get-rich-quick society who say to such a task, "Here am I, use me."

But as I said, there is *nothing* more basic, *nothing* more Christian. If God's people are to be living examples of one thing, that thing ought to be—it must be—compassion. I could not agree more with the late, great preacher John Henry Jowett. When asked what he would emphasize if he had his life to live over, with obvious emotion he replied, "I would major in compassion and comfort."

Chapter 23

A PENETRATING THOUGHT

*A*t times in my life I am seized with a scene from Scripture. Ever had that happen to you? Not long ago it happened to me again.

It was late at night. I clicked the last light out and lowered my head onto the pillow. Outside was a clear, deep blue sky with stars shining brightly through the crisp night air. It was one of those nights when my body had grown tired but my mind wouldn't shift into neutral. I had been reading the Gospel of Matthew and one scene kept passing in review. The night sky added to my imagination, since one day in the future this scene will actually transpire in space, out there where only the stars now reside.

I blinked nervously as the words seemed to burn their way into the windowpane. It seemed so real, I wanted to reach over and feel the inspired etching.

"But when the Son of Man comes in His glory, and all the angels with Him, then He will sit on His glorious throne. And all the nations will be gathered before Him; and He will separate them from one another, as the shepherd separates the sheep from the goats; and He will put the sheep on His right, and the goats on the left" (Matthew 25:31–33). *What an incredible moment that will be,* I mused. *All of humanity will be gathered at that epochal hour before the Savior's throne—sheep and goats alike, separated and awaiting those eternal words from His lips.*

I swallowed hard, blinked again, and forced myself to think through those final words to the sheep. Do you remember them? "Then the King will say to those on His right, 'Come, you who are blessed of My Father, inherit the kingdom prepared for you from the foundation of the world. For I was hungry, and you gave Me something to eat; I was thirsty, and you gave Me drink; I was a stranger, and you invited Me in; naked, and you clothed Me; I was sick, and you visited Me; I was in prison, and you came to Me' " (Matthew 25:34–36).

They will be awestruck, according to the biblical text. They will stare in amazement as they attempt to unravel the mystery of their Lord's hunger and thirst . . . a stranger . . . one who needed clothing as well as a prisoner they visited. Unable to contain their curiosity, they will burst forth with one voice: "Lord, when did we see You hungry, and feed You, or thirsty, and give You drink? And when did we see You a stranger, and invite You in, or naked, and clothe You? And when did we see You sick, or in prison, and come to You?" (vv. 37–39).

His answer blew me away as I lay there staring out the window at the California night.

The King will answer and say to them, "Truly I say to you, to the extent that you did it to one of these brothers of Mine, even the least of them, you did it to Me." (v. 40)

Do you realize what He is saying?

Jesus Christ, our King and Sovereign Lord, will one day invite His own into His glorious kingdom because they demonstrated the authenticity of their faith by the way they treated "the least of these my brothers." Please note that the emphasis is on "the least"—the obscure, the broken, the battered, the unknowns. Not the celebrities. Not the big names. Not the whole-bodied. Not the well-heeled. Not the "beautiful people." Not the prima donnas.

No. But the *least*.

Gloria Hope Hawley, a lady in our former church who is the mother of two mentally handicapped "children" (both of whom are grown but still live at home), slipped the following paraphrase into my hand one night. It pretty well sums up the idea.

It reads, "And He said, 'I was afflicted with cerebral palsy and you listened to my faltering speech and gently held my flailing hands; I was born a Down's syndrome child and you welcomed me into your church. I was retarded and your love reached out to me.' And the people said, 'Lord, when did we see you with cerebral palsy and listen to you, and when were you born with Down's syndrome or retarded?' He said, 'In that you did it to the least of these my people, you did it to me.' "

May I say it again? Christianity doesn't get more basic than that. It is seeing value in, and loving and caring for, and reaching out to, and spending time with, "the least of these." It is doing the unexpected and giving love and care in return for suspicion and hostility.

In a word, it is compassion.

In a nutshell, those words in Matthew's account are saying: If a Christian is Christ and if Christ is compassion . . . then Christianity's finest expression is compassion.

Those were my thoughts that starlit night, and they remain my thoughts to this day. I couldn't agree more with Jeremy Jackson who wrote: "It is a fair rule of thumb that only that love of neighbor which can also draw people to Christ is truly a reflection of that love for God which is its source."[1]

Do you want Christ to be seen in your life? Do you long to have an effective ministry with eternal dimensions? Do you desire to hear King Jesus' voice some future day, inviting you to enjoy the rewards of His kingdom with Him?

Who doesn't? Then I suggest you decide *now* to be different. To risk reaching, without waiting for an invitation to help. Decide now that you are going to invest more of your energy and time on the stripped, the beaten, and the abandoned. They will seldom tell you, but they need to feel His touch through your hands. They are too shy or too proud or too humiliated

> Christianity doesn't get more basic than that. It is doing the unexpected and giving love and care in return for suspicion and hostility.

or too afraid to ask for help, even though they know they're not going to make it on their own. When you allow your compassion to flow freely, you won't need a personal invitation. But like that nameless Samaritan, you will stop, stoop, and serve.

Will it be costly? Yes, sometimes. Notice what author Michael Quoist has to say:

> Lord, why did You tell me to love all men as my brothers?
> I have tried, but I come back to you frightened.
> Lord, I was so peaceful at home, so comfortably settled.
> It was well-furnished, and I felt so cozy.
> I was alone—I was at peace.
> Sheltered from the wind and the rain, kept clean.[2]

Our God wants to dislodge us from our comfortable, smug existence, to move us to mingle with our needy brothers, to stir us to touch those we might otherwise shun. An anonymous poet expressed the challenge well.

> Love has a hem to her garment
> That trails in the very dust;
> It can reach the stains of the streets and lanes,
> And because it can, it must.

Since when did the Christian hold back because something was costly? Or because it brought discomfort? The people in Isaiah's day fell into that very trap, leaving them smug and complacent, massaging a lifeless religion that looked and sounded orthodox, but which in reality lacked substance. The prophet

disturbed them (prophets always do!) by reminding them of
their primary task as the people of God.

> Is this not the fast which I chose,
> To loosen the bonds of wickedness,
> To undo the bands of the yoke,
> And to let the oppressed go free,
> And break every yoke?
> Is it not to divide your bread with the hungry,
> And bring the homeless poor into the house;
> When you see the naked, to cover him;
> And not to hide yourself from your own flesh?
> Then your light will break out like the dawn,
> And your recovery will speedily spring forth;
> And your righteousness will go before you;
> The glory of the LORD will be your rear guard.
> Then you will call, and the LORD will answer;
> You will cry, and He will say, "Here I am."
> If you remove the yoke from your midst,
> The pointing of the finger, and speaking wickedness,
> And if you give yourself to the hungry,
> And satisfy the desire of the afflicted,
> Then your light will rise in darkness,
> and your gloom will become like midday.
> And the LORD will continually guide you,
> And satisfy your desire in scorched places,
> And give strength to your bones;
> And you will be like a watered garden,
> And like a spring of water whose waters do not fail.
> And those from among you will rebuild the ancient ruins;

You will raise up the age-old foundations;
And you will be called the repairer of the breach,
The restorer of the streets in which to dwell.
Isaiah 58:6–12

I don't know of a clearer passage of Scripture on the subject of compassion. Nor do I know of a better way to identify those who do Good Samaritan work than to call them "repairers of the breach" and "restorers of the streets."

Enough of words!

This needy old world has heard such things before. What it longs for is action. Deeds. The real deal. Repairers and restorers at work, in the trenches, doing the things that give us the right to bear the name "Christian." And in the event you grow weary and your resolve to be different starts to wear thin, remember this . . .

There are eyes that are watching. . .

Burning, piercing eyes.

Eyes that miss nothing.

The eyes of the King.

And whatever you do for others in that great King's name, you are doing for Him.

~ •• ~

Christianity's finest expression is

Compassion.

Part Four
Achieve Your Goals:

A Game Plan for Personal Victory

*B*ack when I was in grade school, it was always a special treat when the teacher gave the class permission to do something unusual.

I remember one hot and humid Houston afternoon when she gave everyone the green light to go barefoot after lunch. We got to pull off our socks, stick 'em in our sneakers, and wiggle our toes to our heart's content. During the afternoon recess that extra freedom added great speed to our softball game on the playground.

During my years in the Corps, there were a few times when memos read "Permission Granted" and everybody cheered. Like the time when our Third Division band on Okinawa played late into the night at General Shoup's dress-blues ball . . . and Captain Birch gave us the next two full days off. Nice surprise!

As I look back on the times in my life when someone in authority gave permission to do the unexpected, I cannot recall even once when it wasn't accepted unanimously and enjoyed to the fullest. Nobody in our fifth-grade class even thought of keeping their shoes on during that sweltering afternoon. Guys and gals alike were barefoot inside of five seconds. And I can't recall a single marine asking the captain if he could go ahead and work through those two days of unexpected liberty. *Are you kidding?* We're talking instant acceptance and total enjoyment.

All it took were those two wonderful words, "Permission granted."

Isn't it strange then, now that you and I are grown and have become Christians, how reluctant we are to give ourselves permission . . .

to do . . .

to think . . .

to say . . .

to try . . .

to change . . .

to buy and enjoy . . .

to be different and not worry about who may say what . . .

to reach for goals we've wanted to achieve for years?

"Permission granted." Enjoy! Go after it!

Be Who You Are.

Even though our God has graciously granted us permission to be free, to have liberty, to break the chains of rigidity, and to enjoy so much of this life, many in His family seldom give themselves clearance to take the next step.

The quest for victory stalls before it ever leaves the blocks.

So many use such strange reasoning: "I mean, after all, what would people say?" or "Well, I wasn't raised to enjoy life; I was taught to be more conservative, more responsible, and more serious than that." So goes the persuasion of an oversensitive conscience trained in the school of negativism.

It's tragic. No, worse than that: it is downright unbiblical.

Have we forgotten the promise, "Where the Spirit of the Lord is, there is liberty" (2 Corinthians 3:17)? Let that sink in.

Paul jumped all over the Galatians for allowing a handful of legalistic Judaizers to invade their lives and clip their wings. Remember his rebuke?

> You foolish Galatians, who has bewitched you ... Having begun by the Spirit, are you now being perfected by the flesh? It was for freedom that Christ set us free; therefore keep standing firm and do not be subject again to a yoke of slavery.... For you were called to freedom, brethren. (Galatians 3:1, 3; 5:1, 13)

In other words, "Permission granted." Enjoy! Go after it! Be who you are. Give yourself the okay to break the mold and exercise your God-given freedom. Chase those goals with all your heart.

It may take awhile. And you will have to train yourself to care less and less about what a few may say. It will help if you'll remind yourself that when they criticize you, they simply want you to be as miserable as *they* are. Since they cannot give themselves permission, who do you think you are to get away with it? If you keep that maverick thought in mind, it'll help you soar like an eagle instead of standing around with all the turkeys.

Do you know your biggest hurdle?

You.

It's giving *yourself* permission, plain and simple. If you fail to press on while the light is green, you will spend so much of your life in the amber zone waiting for "just the right moment" or "a time when most people will understand" that you will find yourself on your deathbed surrounded by regrets.

God, in grace, has purchased you from bondage. Christ has literally set you free. The Spirit of the Lord has provided long-awaited liberty—and the indwelling power to go with it. Achievement waits like a new morning, just over that hill where the sun comes up.

Yes, as we have said, you may need to allow time for healing. And yes, it's important to reset your direction, carve out some new goals under the Spirit's direction, and cultivate compassion for those alongside that new path of yours.

But once you've done those things . . . what are you waiting for? Give yourself permission, my friend, to lift those wings and feel the exhilaration of a soaring lifestyle. Pursue those goals with all the strength a loving, mighty God puts within you.

It is the way of victory.

Chapter 24

WE SHALL DO VALIANTLY

o for the gold!" We hear those stirring words every four years as another series of Olympic Games arrives. Talk of winning fills the air. National pride soars to a fever pitch as muscular athletes from around the world seek the chance to redeem their rigorous training. Dreams they have cherished for a lifetime drive them on with fresh determination—hour after hour, day after day.

Each competitor sees in his mind's eye a scene as vivid and real as life itself—a platform built for three, in the background a heavy drumroll, followed by the playing of a majestic national anthem as the athlete's national flag is hoisted. Straight and tall on center stage stands the personification of ecstasy and pride: a champion adorned with a round, gleaming medal hanging from the neck.

It is gold.

The medal represents maximum fulfillment, the ultimate in sports. In that incredible moment, all the world watches with delight as a single athlete embodies what everyone craves—*victory!* All the world may love a lover, but it's certain that it celebrates a victor.

Something deep within all of us longs to win. To come out on top. To achieve an impossible dream. To accomplish some major objective.

But have you noticed something about victory? It's amazingly elusive.

Sometimes we never even begin the quest because we never give ourselves permission. Thoughts of victory seem almost out of reach, belonging, perhaps, to some elite, exclusive class of humanity. We doubt we can win, not only in the physical realm of athletics (how few of us know even one Olympian!), but also in the spiritual realm of day-to-day Christianity. Have you noticed how rare and even remarkable the victorious Christian seems to be?

My hope is that something I say in the closing pages of this book will create the spark you've needed to ignite "the fire in the belly" of a true spiritual champion. The unmistakable qualities of an "overcomer" have lain dormant long enough!

~ •• ~

The Lord our God designed us to be
Victors, not Victims

I am convinced that we Christians have available to us sufficient power to beat the odds. The Lord our God designed us to be victors, not victims. He never commissioned us merely to cope, to grin and bear it, to grind our way along at a snail's pace. No! Instead He has fully equipped us to "overwhelmingly conquer" by the strength of His might. He has granted us full permission to join the ranks of His victorious sons and daughters.

If you're ready to believe that—and allow it to make a difference in your life—then this chapter is meant for you. As you proceed, keep the words of the psalm uppermost in your mind: "Through God we shall do valiantly" (Psalm 60:12).

I suppose if the psalmist had written it today, he would have said, "Through the Lord our God, let's go for the gold!"

Chapter 25

CLEARING THE AIR

*C*hristian books on "victory" are numerous. Browse in a local bookstore and you'll make the same observation. But if you take the time to read those publications, it's likely you'll find yourself more confused than helped.

If it weren't so tragic, I'd find it humorous that so many books on victory leave readers even more defeated and bewildered than before they opened the cover. Some writers tell you to tighten up. Others say to lighten up. A few promote passivity, promising you power if you'll only "let go." Still others insist you need to "take up" special armor or "put off" the flesh.

Or hold on longer.

Or try harder.

Or reach higher.

Or pray a particular formula.

Or fan your emotions into flame.

Invariably, a few chide you for not "living above this world." Others, with equal vigor, hold out the promise of financial abundance ("God wants you to be rich!") if you only will avail yourself of some special prescription for blessing (as in, "Send me your next paycheck").

Is it any wonder that real victory seems elusive? Confusion and conquest cannot coexist.

We need to clear the air of as much theological smog as possible. To do that, let's savor one of the greatest, most victorious passages in all of the New Testament . . . and all of literature, for that matter. Let these ringing words stir you afresh.

What then shall we say to these things? If God is for us, who is against us? He who did not spare His own Son, but delivered Him up for us all, how will He not also with Him freely give us all things? Who will bring a charge against God's elect? God is the one who justifies; who is the one who condemns? Christ Jesus is He who died, yes, rather who was raised, who is at the right hand of God, who also intercedes for us. Who shall separate us from the love of Christ? Shall tribulation, or

> Is it any wonder that real victory seems elusive?
> Confusion and Conquest Cannot Coexist.

distress, or persecution, or famine, or nakedness, or peril, or sword? Just as it is written,

"For Thy sake we are being put to death all day long;
We were considered as sheep to be slaughtered."

But in all these things we overwhelmingly conquer through Him who loved us. (Romans 8:31–37)

What a potent slice of Scripture! Look closely with me at these seven triumphant verses. The passage features one question after another, each calling forth a bold, confident answer.

I confess that I cannot read these words without smiling. Without fail, they lift my spirit. What assurance! Such confidence! And did you notice the climactic ending? *"We overwhelmingly conquer."* Talk about winning!

But wait. The context of these bold statements sounds anything but victorious. Where are the triumphant soldiers with fixed bayonets, the flying banners, the smoking cannons? Look again at who's pictured here and try not to be surprised. Do you see them?

Sheep. Sheep ready to be slaughtered!

Now, how is *that* a picture of victory? Seems more like a snapshot of a bustling butcher shop!

And the picture doesn't seem to get any better even when we look more closely. The phrase, "the spoils of victory," doesn't normally prompt a mental image of the sort of battlefield envisioned here. We see tribulation. Affliction. Pain. Hardship. Loss. Hunger. Danger. Even death.

Where are the impressive displays of power? Where are the trophies we usually associate with success and victory?

I'll be honest. They're not there. Instead, we find oceans of inner strength, seas of unfailing determination, worlds of quiet confidence, solid security, and unswerving love. It is in and through these things that we "overwhelmingly conquer."

Victory, it seems, is not at all what we might expect. Have you noticed how the word *unexpected* has popped up several times in this book? For whatever reason, that seems to be the way our God delights to work in this world.

By unexpected means . . . through unexpected people . . . in unexpected ways . . . at unexpected times. We shouldn't be surprised then to learn that His definition of "victory" doesn't square with the common understanding.

Let me show you what I mean. . . .

His definition of "victory" doesn't square with the common understanding.

Chapter 26

FOUR THINGS
VICTORY IS NOT

Victory is not a once-for-all, automatic inheritance.

Christians need to be reminded that the life God provides—commonly called the "abundant life"—is not a continuous, unbroken chain of victories. Victory is available, but it is not automatic. The strength we need to handle life's pressures is there to be claimed, but we should never think of the Christian life as "instant success."

Victory is not an emotional high.

You'll look in vain for a list of "feelings" in Romans 8. On the contrary, you'll find statements of assurance, strong affirmation, and confidence-building. Christians do not gain victory by psyching themselves up or getting in the mood.

Victory is not a dream reserved for supersaints.

Unlike the lonely runner on the track, the Christian who conquers does so "through Him who loved us." Or, as we read elsewhere, "Thanks be to God, who gives us the victory through our Lord Jesus Christ" (1 Corinthians 15:57).

Victory does not happen to us while we passively wait.

I cannot think of a more subtle adversary of victory than passivity. Many today peddle a spiritual-sounding version of the "sit and wait" philosophy, and unfortunately they find eager multitudes ready to drink their poison. Yet a familiar axiom remains as true today as when it was first stated: "To the victor belong the responsibilities."

We may be compared to sheep and we may find it essential to draw upon our Lord for the perseverance and the power

~ •• ~

The victorious Christian,
like the victorious athlete,
wins because he or she is deliberately
and personally involved
—from start to finish—
in a process that leads to victory.

we need, but *the victory we desire is never automatic.* Passivity is an enemy to anyone who hopes to live a life of victory. It's as foolish for the believer to think that conquering will "just happen" as it would be to imagine an Olympic champion standing on the winner's platform and claiming, "I really had nothing to do with this gold medal. Just a few minutes ago I looked down and there it was, hanging around my neck."

What a joke! The victorious Christian, like the victorious athlete, wins because he or she is deliberately and personally involved—from start to finish—in a process that leads to victory.

Make no mistake about it, spiritual victory doesn't come like a box of detergent in a new washing machine. If you are to achieve your goals, you must be involved to the maximum extent.

But enough of the negatives! Let's spend the balance of our time thinking about the positives—the specifics involved in a life marked by victory.

Chapter 27

FOUR ELEMENTS
OF VICTORY

can think of no better scripture on victory than the final four verses of 1 Corinthians 9—a passage rippling with muscle. Its words throb with athletic determination. "Do you not know that those who run in a race all run, but only one receives the prize? Run in such a way that you may win. And everyone who competes in the games exercises self-control in all things. They then do it to receive a perishable wreath, but we an imperishable. Therefore I run in such a way, as not without aim; I box in such a way, as not beating the air; but I buffet my body and make it my slave, lest possibly, after I have preached to others, I myself should be disqualified" (1 Corinthians 9:24–27).

I have thought about the words of this passage for years. I can remember reading and rereading them in my thumb-worn *Amplified Bible* while I was in the marines on Okinawa.

Yet to this day, the more I meditate on these verses, the more significant they become to me.

It's almost as though the great apostle Paul is giving us his personal credo. I believe this is a condensed version of how the man was able to stay on track in spite of challenges that would have buckled the knees of most of us. What a spiritual champion!

I find here at least four essentials that lead to a life of victory—action, aim, discipline, and reward. Let's take a closer look at each.

ACTION

These verses drip with the sweat of an athlete. You can almost hear the grunts and feel the perspiration—those agonizing marks of the track, the court, the ring. Paul weaves enthusiasm throughout the fabric of his words. Picture the action as you read.

Verse 24:   "Those who run in a race . . ."
                 "Run . . . that you may win."

∼ •• ⌣

I find here at least four essentials that lead to a life of victory—

Action, Aim, Discipline, and Reward.

Verse 25:	"Everyone who competes in the games exercises self-control in all things."
Verse 26:	"I run . . . I box."
Verse 27:	"I buffet my body and make it my slave."

The mention of "the games" in verse 25 intrigues me, especially because of Paul's use of a Greek term translated "competes" in the same verse. The term is *agonizomai,* the very word from which we get our English words "agony" and "agonize." Whatever "games" the apostle had in mind involved "agonizing competition."

Athletic contests were common in the Greek world. Not only did the Greeks hold their Olympics, but every three years they flocked into the stadiums in ancient Corinth to witness the Isthmian Games as well. As is true today, all the athletes in those ancient games underwent a strict training program for many long months.

The games featured various athletic contests, including running—both short dashes and lengthy marathons—and an event called "leaping"—much like our long jump, no doubt. In addition, spectators watched spear throwing (answering, perhaps, to the javelin today), wrestling, boxing, chariot racing, and even racing in armor, plus other competitions.

In order to qualify for the games of ancient Greece, athletes were obligated to take an oath stating that they had trained for at least ten months. They also swore they would not resort to any deceitful or unfair "tricks."

Those ancient athletes watched their diets with great care and dedicated themselves to workout regimens nothing short of excruciating. With earnestness of purpose and self-sacrificial resolve, they trained wholeheartedly for the games.

To the sports-minded Greek, the gymnasium became the center of the universe. He saturated his life with the spirit of competition. The action-oriented society of the ancient Greeks more closely resembled our own active, fitness-crazed lifestyle than most of us would ever believe.

And it's with that kind of world in mind that Paul writes of victory.

At the risk of repetition overkill, may I remind you that a life characterized by victory is not a laid-back life? It is rather an active, even aggressive, pursuit.

A number of years ago, at the close of a speaking engagement, an elderly gentleman caught my attention. He was chatting with several folks in the back of the auditorium, looked at me as I walked by, and with a grin and a twinkle in his eye, whipped out his hand—a hand you could strike a match on, toughened by decades of rugged toil.

"You look like a man who enjoys life," I said. "What do you do for a living?"

"Me? Well, I'm a farmer from back in the Midwest."

"Really? I guess I'm not surprised, since you've got hands like a tractor tire."

He laughed, asked me a couple of insightful questions, then told me about his plans for traveling on his own through the western states.

"What did you do last week?" I asked. His answer stunned me. "Last week I finished harvesting ninety thousand bushels of corn," he said with a smile.

"Ninety thousand! How old are you, my friend?"

He didn't seem at all hesitant or embarrassed by my question. "I'm just a couple months shy o' ninety." He laughed again as I shook my head.

He had lived through four wars, the Great Depression, sixteen presidents, ninety Midwest winters, who knows how many personal hardships . . . and still he was taking life by the throat.

I had to ask him the secret of his long and productive life. "Hard work and integrity," came his quick reply.

As we parted company, he looked back over his shoulder and offered a striking variation of the usual parting comment.

"Don't take it easy, young feller. Stay at it!"

Good words for all of us! No one ever harvested a crop by playing solitaire on the front porch or by watching reruns of *Gilligan's Island*. No one ever won an Indy 500 by popping his car into cruise control and driving with one hand on the wheel while sipping a diet soda. Victory belongs to those who are engaged—those who put it in gear and start moving.

This brings us to the next essential in a life of victory—*aim*.

AIM

Read a few more statements and phrases from 1 Corinthians 9:

Verse 24:	"All run, but only one receives the prize. Run in such a way that you may win."
Verse 26:	"I run in such a way, as not without aim; I box in such a way, as not beating the air."

Any runner who wants to win must stay on course. The victorious competitor locks his or her eye on the final tape. Those who run, aim at the finish line. The same is true of a boxer. If we were to put verse 26 in today's terms, we'd say, "I box, but I don't shadowbox!" As one authority describes it, "'no air-smiter': he uses his fists as one in deadly earnest, and does not miss: he plants his blow."[1]

Paul's point is clear. The Christian faces a host of very real enemies. Few have pictured them more clearly than John Bunyan in *The Pilgrim's Progress*. Foe after foe relentlessly fell upon Christian, bringing along his own subtle snare. If Christian were to make it to the Celestial City, he needed to keep his aim clear. Losing sight of the goal—mere "shadowboxing"—would only disrupt his walk. So it is with all of us in the evil days at the turn of the millennium.

Someone once said, "So far from the world being a goddess in petticoats, it is rather a devil in a strait waistcoat." It's true. Our world is downright devilish, full of potholes, traps, and subtle snares designed to bump the Christian off course. Long enough have we courted its fancy and returned the smile of its alluring face! The believer who aims to love God and to live victoriously for Christ must get tough and decide to stand alone, when necessary.

> Any runner who wants to win must stay on course.

Isaac Watts put it this way:

> Am I a soldier of the cross,
> A follower of the Lamb?
> And shall I fear to own His cause,
> Or blush to speak His name?
> Are there no foes for me to face?
> Must I not stem the flood?
> Is this vile world a friend to grace,
> To help me on to God?

Good questions, those. Tough-minded, sinewy questions. Those who choose to walk in victory must answer them almost daily—sometimes hourly.

It helps me to set goals. To achieve anything significant in my life, I find I must first determine a set of objectives. As I reach each objective, I move systematically closer to my ultimate goal. This goal-setting philosophy or mind-set is what I mean by aim.

Victory requires it. Why? Because victory isn't discovered, it is *achieved*. Troops don't stumble into winning a battle; their triumph results from a thoughtful strategy, a carefully crafted plan of attack.

The same analogy holds true for a ball game. High-priced, brilliant, seasoned coaches spend hours every week thinking about and then communicating their game plan. Players who enter the contest must have memorized the plan. To use Paul's words, they "run in such a way, as not without aim."

May I be so bold as to ask, where are you going? How do you plan to get there? What's your strategy for achieving maximum life influence without losing the balance of com-passion? Even more specifically, what is your game plan for handling the temptations you are sure to face? I am con-vinced that these and related questions must be asked and answered if we hope to be among the ranks of those who "overwhelmingly conquer."

Sound too tight? Too rigid? You're wondering if even Paul lived with such a well-crafted game plan? We find the answers to those questions in the words he wrote from prison shortly before he was beheaded. He said, "For I am already being poured out as a drink offering, and the time of my departure has come. I have fought the good fight, I have finished the course, I have kept the faith" (2 Timothy 4:6–7).

Aim and victory walk in step with each other. But equally important for a life of victory is discipline.

DISCIPLINE

Discipline is one of the most hated terms of our times . . . right alongside *patience* and *self-control*. But have you noticed how often it comes up in the testimonies of those who win?

Victory isn't discovered,
it is Achieved.

The great apostle says that he willingly forfeited his apostolic rights for the sake of winning more (1 Corinthians 9:19–23). That took discipline. In 2 Timothy 2:10, he mentions that he endured all things in order to reach his objective. That certainly took discipline. As we read earlier in 1 Corinthians 9:25, Paul says that those who compete in the games exercise "self-control in all things." Again, discipline is key.

- No runner completes the training or a race without it.
- No weight-loss program is maintained without it.
- No human body is kept fit without it.
- No mind is sharpened without it.
- No temptation is overcome without it.

So who are we kidding? Without discipline, we can kiss victory good-bye. We can forget about achieving our goals. And the alternative to discipline skims dangerously close to an irresponsible lifestyle (hardly the model of an authentic Christian). This came home to me forcefully when I read a statement that originally appeared in the *Wheaton College Bulletin*.

> The undisciplined is a headache to himself and a heartache to others, and is unprepared to face the stern realities of life.

If you want to put a stop to mediocrity, to replace excuses with fresh determination and procrastination with tough-minded perseverance, you need discipline. Winners know that disciplined persistence must be a major part of their training. That's the only way victory becomes an attainable reality rather than a distant dream.

The late Ray Kroc, founder of the world-famous

McDonald's hamburger chain, loved the same statement that football coach Vince Lombardi often quoted: "Press on: Nothing in the world can take the place of persistence. Talent will not; nothing is more common than unsuccessful individuals with talent. Genius will not; unrewarded genius is almost a proverb. Education will not; the world is full of educated derelicts. Persistence and determination alone are omnipotent."[2]

Before you are tempted to think, *I'm too old to start now,* remember that Kroc didn't start McDonald's until he was fifty-two! And lest you assume a late start offers few benefits, recall that he reached the billion-dollar mark in just twenty-two years. By contrast, it took IBM forty-six years to reach its first billion; Xerox took sixty-two years. So starting late could have its advantages!

But wait. We're not talking about making money; we're talking about building a life. The subject is victory—personal victory, becoming an individual with a will to win, a person who draws upon the limitless power of the living God to face life head-on, regardless of the challenges.

One of the many exciting aspects of my years of ministry—whether as the pastor of a church or the president of a seminary—has been to witness the spiritual growth of those under my care. Sometimes the ones who grow the fastest and become the best models of strength and determination are those with extremely difficult circumstances.

One such individual comes to mind from our former church in Southern California. A single parent, the product of an abusive home and intense marital conflicts, emotionally starved, this young woman stumbled into our fellowship and found encouragement, support, and hope. Christ became her

Savior and her never-failing Friend. She went through long months of professional counseling with a dedicated Christian therapist.

With an indomitable will to go on, she began to drink in the Scriptures. She opened her arms to others in need. She became an authentic, flesh-and-blood example of remarkable change—the kind of change only God could inspire. In place of moral compromise, she began to live in purity. Instead of insecurity and low self-esteem, she began to believe in herself . . . to see worth and value in her life.

She became victorious!

In a letter of gratitude she wrote years ago, she mentioned the importance of discipline (or persistence, as she called it): "Without persistence I would be dead. I would have given in to the despair of hopelessness that was my life. I would have surely died from loneliness. . . . Victory is the result."

Then she added: "This has been another incredibly challenging year as a mother of two teenagers, as a single parent, as a student of psychology at Cal State Fullerton. I graduate next May and then want to go on to get my masters and MFCC license. Talk about persistence! If I hadn't had it, I'd have buckled under a long time ago."

Isn't that magnificent! If only you could have watched the change in this lady as Cynthia and I did. Graduating from college in the spring, she went on to lose twenty unwanted pounds the following summer. What determination!

Is setting such goals worth it? I mean, in the final analysis, does that kind of tough-minded determination pay off? The answer is clear when we look at the crowning point of all—*reward,* the fourth essential in a life of victory.

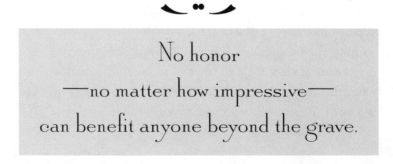
REWARD

It's never a bad thing to remind ourselves of the prize awaiting those who live to please God. Paul often did that, which is one huge reason he was able to keep going even when giving up would have been easier. "They then do it to receive a perishable wreath, but we an imperishable" (1 Corinthians 9:25).

I'm not sure that so few words ever carried greater meaning. The contrast is nothing short of phenomenal. The "they" refers to the athletes who strain, sweat, train, and finally win . . . a wreath that browns, withers, gets tossed away, and is soon forgotten.

Oh, it's true the athlete received a few other perks. A herald proclaimed the victor's name as well as his home. The winner received five hundred drachmae from Athens, a triumphal entrance into his hometown, and a perpetual seat of honor at all succeeding games. Tradition tells us that the winner's children were educated free of charge, and he was relieved of taxation and military duty for the rest of his life . . . as he basked in the fame that followed the victor all his days.[3]

Yet all this was destined to perish. Nothing the victor gained carried lasting value or an eternal dimension.

No honor
—no matter how impressive—
can benefit anyone beyond the grave.

That's still true today. There is no trophy that will not ultimately settle into dust. Champion boxers wear the jeweled belt only temporarily—until another world champion is crowned. No Super Bowl ring resists tarnishing, no honor—no matter how impressive—can benefit anyone beyond the grave. All the applause, all the ink from sportswriters' pens, all the talk (from small cafés to swanky, sophisticated clubs (will soon fade. The best that can be said for the athlete's prize is that it's "a perishable wreath."

Not so for the Christian conqueror! Our victory wreath is designated by God as "imperishable." Flip back to 1 Corinthians 3 and note with me three primary facts regarding these heavenly rewards.

Most Rewards Are Received in Heaven, Not on Earth

Now don't misunderstand. There *are* earthly rewards. But God reserves special honors for that day when "each man's work will become evident" and "he shall receive a reward" (3:13–14).

All Rewards Are Based on Quality, Not Quantity

Size and volume and noise and numbers impress us humans. Too easily we forget that God's eye fixes on motive. When He rewards His servants, He does so based on quality—which means everybody has an equal opportunity to receive a reward. The elderly woman who prays before an audience of One will be rewarded as much as the evangelist who preaches before an audience of thousands.

No Postponed Reward Will Be Forgotten

God doesn't settle accounts at the end of every day. Nor does He close out His books toward the end of everyone's life. But when that day in eternity dawns, when time shall be no more, no act of serving others—be it well-known or obscure—will be forgotten. Unlike many people today, God keeps His promises.

Someone once counted every biblical promise and came up with an amazing figure of almost 7,500. Servants can claim many of those promises even today. Believe me, there are times when the only thing that keeps me going is a promise from God that my work is not in vain.

When we have done what was needed but were ignored, misunderstood, or forgotten, we can be sure our labor was not in vain.

When we did what was right, with the right motive, but received no credit, no acknowledgement, not even a "thank you" . . . we have God's promise that "we shall reap."

When any servant has served and given and sacrificed and then willingly stepped aside for God to receive the glory, our heavenly Father promises he will "receive back."

Among our temporal rewards is the *quiet awareness that the life of Christ is being modeled.* I know of few more satisfying and encouraging rewards than to realize that our actions can become visible expressions of Christ to others.

Another temporal reward is the *joyful realization that a thankful spirit is being stimulated:* "All this is for your benefit, so that the grace that is reaching more and more people may cause thanksgiving to overflow to the glory of God" (2 Corinthians 4:15, NIV).

And then there are the eternal rewards! The Bible refers to some of them as "crowns," set aside for God's servants. God's Word speaks of at least five crowns.

The imperishable crown (1 Corinthians 9:24–27)

This reward will be awarded to those believers who consistently bring the flesh under the Holy Spirit's control and refuse to be enslaved by their sinful nature.

The crown of exultation
(Philippians 4:1; 1 Thessalonians 2:19–20)

Our Lord will distribute this crown to those servants who are faithful to declare the gospel, lead souls to Christ, and build them up in Him.

The crown of righteousness (2 Timothy 4:7–8)

This crown will be awarded to those who live each day with eternity's values in view, anticipating Christ's imminent return.

There are times when the only thing that keeps me going is a promise from God that

My work is not in vain.

The crown of life (James 1:12)

This crown is promised not to those who endure suffering and trials, but to those who endure their trials while loving the Savior all the way.

The crown of glory (1 Peter 5:1–4)

This reward is promised to those who faithfully "shepherd the flock" in keeping with the requirements spelled out in verses 2–3 of 1 Peter 5.

If I correctly read God's plan for our future, I note that those saints "crowned" for walking in victory will, one day in glory, "fall down before Him who sits on the throne, and will worship Him who lives forever and ever, and will cast their crowns before the throne, saying, 'Worthy art Thou, our Lord and our God, to receive glory and honor and power; for Thou didst create all things, and because of Thy will they existed, and were created' " (Revelation 4:10–11).

What a scene! All God's servants kneel before His throne. Are they strutting around heaven displaying their crowns? No. They have cast them at the feet of the Worthy One . . . the Victorious King, who invites His redeemed sons and daughters to revel in that victory forever.

There are times in my life when I close my eyes and try to imagine such a scene. When I do, I often recall the words of a grand old hymn of the church which is seldom sung these days—"The Sands of Time" by Anne R. Cousin.

The sands of time are sinking,
The dawn of heaven breaks;
The summer morn I've sighed for,
The fair, sweet morn awakes;
Dark, dark hath been the midnight,
But dayspring is at hand,
And glory, glory dwelleth
In Immanuel's land.

The Bride eyes not her garment,
But her dear Bridegroom's face;
I will not gaze at glory
But on my King of grace.
Not at the crown He giveth
But on His pierced hand,
The Lamb is all the glory
Of Immanuel's land.

If all we had to keep us going were the sweat and grind of a hot track or the demanding hours and sacrificial diet of a relentless training schedule, it's doubtful any of us could make it. Victory would, indeed, be only a dream for supermen and wonder-women. But God promises His people a reward that will never perish.

Who wouldn't want such a reward? Compared to God's eternal benefits, who would ever opt for the temporary?

But how? How is it possible for mere human beings to connect with such eternal values? What is truly necessary for a life of victory?

Chapter 28

SIMPLE REQUIREMENTS FOR VICTORY

ccording to Scripture, three things are required for spiritual victory: Birth, faith, and truth. "For whatever is born of God overcomes the world; and this is the victory that has overcome the world—our faith. And who is the one who overcomes the world, but he who believes that Jesus is the Son of God? It is the Spirit who bears witness, because the Spirit is the truth" (1 John 5:4–5, 7).

In order to enter into the ranks of the victorious, we must be "born of God." Jesus called this process being "born anew" and/or being "born again." It occurs when I accept the gift of eternal life made possible by Jesus' death and resurrection . . . when I, personally, ask the Son of God to become my Savior from sin. Birth must precede everything. With it I receive Christ's life, power, and cleansing.

Then comes faith. I draw upon the power that is in me. I no

longer operate on the basis of human strength, but by faith, I rely upon divine power. The difference in the two is like that between rumbling along in a twenty-five-ton tank and lifting off the runway in a Phantom jet.

Look again at what was said in 1 John 5:4: "And this is the victory that has overcome the world—our faith."

Everything is made possible by the truth. By believing the truth. Living the truth. Allowing the truth to invade, reshape, and cultivate our lives anew.

Tell me, have you had such a birth?

If so, are you operating on faith?

And the truth—is it the truth you are claiming?

If you've answered yes to all three questions, then it's time for action. Quit hiding behind those excuses! Stop telling yourself it's too late! It is never too late to start doing what is right. Start now. The alternative is too grim to consider. Trust me, you can move from the realm of defeat and discouragement to victory and hope if you will simply take action now.

Aim high.

Go hard after God.

Press on.

Everything is made possible by the truth.

By believing the truth.

Living the truth.

Chapter 29

PRESSING ON

*F*lying ace Chuck Yeager wrote a book some years ago with the inviting title: *Press On!* A guy with his adventurous background, plus a chest full of medals to prove his mettle, probably has a lot to say about "pressing on."

Few of us will ever know the thrill of breaking speed records or sound barriers, but all of us live with the daily challenge of pressing on. The question is how.

How does the widow or widower go on after the flowers wilt and the grass begins to grow over the grave?

How does the athlete go on after age or injury takes its toll and someone younger takes his or her place?

How does the mother go on after the children grow up and no longer need her?

How does the victim move beyond the abuse or injustice without turning bitter?

How does the patient go on after the physician breaks the news about the dreaded biopsy?
How does the divorcee go on after the divorce is final?
How does anyone press on when the bottom drops out?
What's the secret?

I'm not sure I would call it a secret, but I have recently discovered some principles from Scripture that have certainly come to my rescue. They emerge from the life of David during a period where he found himself unable to escape tough times.

David and his fellow warriors were returning from battle. Exhausted, dirty, and anxious to get home, they came upon a scene that took their breath away. Where once lay their own quiet village, they found nothing but smoldering ruins. Their wives and children? Kidnapped by the same enemy that had burned their homes to the ground. Their initial reactions? "Then David and the people who were with him lifted their voices and wept until there was no strength in them to weep" (1 Samuel 30:4).

Bad enough. But it gets worse.

In the bitter aftermath of that shock, David's own men turned against him. Talk of mutiny swirled among the soldiers. "Moreover David was greatly distressed because the people spoke of stoning him, for all the people were embittered, each one because of his sons and his daughters" (30:6).

Those descriptive words, "greatly distressed," represent deep anguish and intense depression. If ever a man felt like hanging it up, David must have in those agonizing moments.

But he didn't.

What did he do instead? Read this very carefully: "But David strengthened himself in the LORD his God" (1 Samuel 30:6).

David got alone and "gave himself a good talking to," as my mother used to say. He poured out his heart before the Lord . . . got things squared away vertically, which helped clear away the fog horizontally. He did not surrender to the hard times.

Why not? How did he go on?

By refusing to focus on the present situation only.

What happens when we stay riveted to the present misery? One of two things: either we blame someone (which can easily make us bitter), or we submerge in self-pity (which paralyzes us). We will never go on with our lives as long as we concentrate all our attention on our present pain.

Instead of retaliating or curling up in a corner and licking his wounds, David called to mind that this, even this, was no mistake. The Lord hadn't skipped town. On the contrary, He was in full control. Bruised and bloody, David faced the test head-on and refused to throw in the towel.

And the victory began that very afternoon!

We will never go on with our lives as long as we concentrate all our attention on our present pain.

Chapter 30

A PORTRAIT
OF DETERMINATION

*W*henever I think about pressing on, about pursuing goals and reaching for victory in the face of intolerable odds, the name of Wilma Rudolph pops up in my mind.

Born prematurely, Wilma contracted double pneumonia (twice) and scarlet fever. The worst was a bout with polio, which left her with a crooked left leg and a foot twisted inward. Metal leg braces, stares from neighborhood kids, and six years of bus rides to Nashville for treatments could have driven this young girl into a self-made shell.

But Wilma refused.

Wilma kept dreaming.

She was determined not to allow her disability to get in the way of her dreams. Maybe her determination was generated by the faith of her Christian mother, who often said, "Honey, the most important thing in life is for you to believe it and keep on trying."

By age eleven, Wilma decided to "believe it." And through sheer determination and an indomitable spirit to persevere, *regardless,* she forced herself to learn how to walk without the braces.

At age twelve she made a wonderful discovery: Girls could run and jump and play ball just like boys! Her older sister Yvonne was quite good at basketball, so Wilma decided to challenge her on the court. She began to improve. The two of them ultimately went out for the same school team. Yvonne made the final twelve, but Wilma didn't. But because her father wouldn't allow Yvonne to travel with the team without her sister as a chaperone, Wilma found herself often in the presence of the coach.

One day she built up enough nerve to confront the man with her magnificent obsession—her lifetime dream. She blurted out, "If you will give me ten minutes of your time every day—and only ten minutes—I will give you a world-class athlete."

He took her up on the offer. The result is history. Young Wilma finally won a starting position on the basketball squad; and when that season ended, she decided to try out for the track team. What a decision!

In her first race, she beat her girlfriend. Then she beat all the girls in her high school . . . then, *every* high-school girl in the state of Tennessee. Wilma was only fourteen, but already a champion.

Shortly thereafter, although still in high school, she was invited to join the Tigerbelle's track team at Tennessee State University. She began a serious training program after school and on weekends. As she improved, she continued winning short dashes and the 440-yard relay.

Two years later she was invited to try out for the Olympics. She qualified and ran in the 1956 games at Melbourne, Australia. She won a bronze medal as her team placed third in the 400-meter relay, a bittersweet victory. She had won—but she decided that next time she would "go for the gold."

I could skip four years and hurry on to Rome, but that would not do justice to the whole story. Wilma realized that victory would require an enormous amount of commitment, sacrifice, and discipline. To give her "the winner's edge" as a world-class athlete, she began a do-it-yourself program similar to the one she had employed to get herself out of those leg braces. Not only did she run at six and ten every morning and at three every afternoon, she would often sneak down the dormitory fire escape from eight to ten o'clock and run on the track before bedtime. Week after week, month in and month out, Wilma maintained the same grueling schedule . . . for over twelve hundred days.

Now we're ready for Rome. When the sleek, trim, young black lady, only twenty years old, walked out onto the field, she was ready. She had paid the price. Even those eighty thousand fans could sense the spirit of victory. It was electrifying. As she began her warm-up sprints, a cadenced chant began to emerge from the stands: "Vilma . . . Vilma . . . VILMA!" The crowd was as confident as she that she could win.

And win she did.

She breezed to an easy victory in the 100-meter dash. Then she won the 200-meter dash. And finally, she anchored the U.S. women's team to another first-place finish in the 400-meter relay. Three gold medals—the first woman in history to win three gold medals in track and field. I should add that each of the three races was won in world-record time.[1]

The little crippled girl from Clarksville, Tennessee, was now a world-class athlete. Wilma Rudolph had decided she couldn't allow her disability to disqualify her; instead, she chose to pay the price for victory and "go for the gold."

Christ offers us a winning game plan for life. It is not a distant dream, but a present reality. As He comes into our lives, He brings all the power we will ever need, all the confidence, all the hope, all the determination, everything. He, the Ultimate Victor, smiles with affirmation and applauds our every determination to draw upon His all-sufficiency.

If Wilma Rudolph could muster the courage to shed those leg braces and overcome one hurdle after another in her pursuit of the gold, I am convinced we can too. And the kind of gold God promises us will never tarnish, never diminish in significance, never fade away.

If you are ready, I'll run with you. Let's begin today.

Christ offers us a winning game plan for life.

MAKE ME THY FUEL

From prayer that asks that I may be
Sheltered from winds that beat on Thee,
From fearing when I should aspire,
From faltering when I should climb higher,
From silken self, O Captain, free
Thy soldier who would follow Thee.

From subtle love of softening things,
From easy choices, weakenings,
Not thus are spirits fortified,
Not this way went the Crucified,
From all that dims Thy Calvary,
O Lamb of God, deliver me.

Give me the love that leads the way,
The faith that nothing can dismay,
The hope no disappointments tire,
The passion that will burn like fire,
Let me not sink to be a clod:
Make me Thy fuel, Flame of God.[2]

—Amy Carmichael

ENDNOTES

Chapter One

1. Charles R. Swindoll, *Finishing Touch* (Dallas, TX.: Word Publishing, 1994).

Chapter Four

1. Winston S. Churchill, "Pointing as a Pastime," an essay from the book *A Man of Destiny* compiled by the editors of Country Beautiful (Waukesha, WI: Country Beautiful Foundation, Inc., 1965), 63.

Chapter Five

1. Archibald Thomas Robertson, *Word Pictures in the New Testament,* Vol. III, The Acts of the Apostles (Nashville, TN: Broadman Press, 1930), 480.

Chapter Six

1. Everett F. Harrison, ed. *The Wycliffe Bible Commentary* (Chicago, IL: Moody Press, 1962), 1176.

Chapter Ten

1. Frank Goble, *The Men at the Top* (Thornwood, NY: Caroline House Publishers, 1972), 67.

Chapter Twelve

1. Ted W. Engstrom, *The Making of a Christian Leader* (Grand Rapids, MI: Zondervan Publishing House, 1976), 67.

Chapter Fourteen

1. Gordon MacDonald, *Facing Turbulent Times* (Wheaton, IL: Tyndale House Publisher, Inc., 1981), 93.
2. Dwight Eisenhower, "Leadership," *Quote Unquote,* Lloyd Cory, ed. (Wheaton, IL: Victor Books, a division of SP Publications, Inc., 1977), 177.
3. Anne Morrow Lindbergh, *Gift from the Sea* (New York, NY: Pantheon Publisher, a division of Random House, 1955), 23–24.
4. Lee Iacocca, *Iacocca: An Autobiography* (New York, NY: Bantam Books, 1984), 146.
5. Paul Martin, "Greed," *Quote Unquote,* Lloyd Cory, ed. (Wheaton, IL: Victor Books, a division of SP Publications, Inc., 1977).
6. Gordon MacDonald, 103.
7. Ibid.

Chapter Fifteen

1. James C. Dobson, *Straight Talk to Men and Their Wives* (Waco, TX: Word Books, 1980), 96.

2. *Man of Steel and Velvet* address by Carl Sandburg given before Eighty-sixth Congress, first session, 12 February 1959, Vol. 105, 2265–2266.

Chapter Sixteen
1. Howard Rutledge and Phyllis Rutledge with Mel White and Lyla White, *In the Presence of Mine Enemies* (Old Tappan, NJ: Fleming H. Revell, 1973), 34.

Chapter Seventeen
1. A statement made by Dr. Carl F. H. Henry in a speech at the National Religious Broadcaster Convention in Washington, D.C. in January, 1983. Dr. Henry's source for the Niebuhr story was Dr. Ben Armstrong of NRB.

Chapter Eighteen
1. William M. Fletcher, *The Second Greatest Commandment* (Colorado Springs, CO: NavPress, 1983), 57–58.

Chapter Nineteen
1. Walter Tubbs, "Beyond Pearls," *Journal of Humanistic Psychology*, Vol. 12, No. 2 (1972), 5. Reprinted by permission of Saga Publications, Inc.

Chapter Twenty
1. From the book, *Glad to Be Me,* edited by Dov Peretz Elkins, ©1976 by Prentice-Hall, Inc., 28-29.

Published by Prentice-Hall, Inc., Englewood Cliffs, NJ 07632.

Chapter Twenty-Two
1. Jess Moody, *Quote Unquote*, Lloyd Cory, ed. (Wheaton, IL: Victor Books, a division of SP Publications, Inc., 1977), 66.
2. Ruth Harms Calkin, *Tell Me Again, Lord, I Forget* (Elgin, IL: David C. Cook Publishing Co., 1974), 14. Used by permission of the author.

Chapter Twenty-Three
1. Jeremy C. Jackson, *No Other Foundation* (Westchester, IL: Cornerstone Books, 1980), 283.
2. Michael Quiost, quoted by William M. Fletcher in *The Second Greatest Commandment* (Colorado Springs, CO: NavPress, 1984), 43.

Chapter Twenty-Seven
1. Archibald Robertson and Alfred Plummer, *A Critical and Exegetical Commentary on the First Epistle of St. Paul to the Corinthians,* The International Critical Commentary (Edinburgh, England: T. & T. Clark, 1914), 196.
2. Ray A. Kroc, *Grinding It Out* (New York, NY: Berkley, 1978), 201.
3. Merrill F. Unger, *Unger's Bible Dictionary* (Chicago: Moody Press, 1957), 389.

Chapter Thirty

1. Wilma Rudolph, *Wilma: The Story of Wilma Rudolph*, ed. Bud Greenspan (New York: New American Library, Inc., 1977).

2. Amy Carmichael, *"Make Me Thy Fuel,"* in *Toward Jerusalem*, used by permission of Christian Literature Crusade, Inc., Fort Washington, PA, and S.P.C.K., Holy Trinity Church, London.